JOURNEY OF SHADOWS

A TALE OF SURVIVAL AND REDEMPTION

MICHAEL KELLY

Journey of Shadows

Copyright © 2025 by Michael Kelly.

All rights reserved. No part of this publication may be reproduced, distributed, or transmitted in any form or by any means, including photocopying, recording, or other electronic or mechanical methods, without the written consent of the publisher. The only exceptions are for brief quotations included in critical reviews and other noncommercial uses permitted by copyright law.

MILTON & HUGO L.L.C.
4407 Park Ave., Suite 5
Union City, NJ 07087, USA

Website: *www.miltonandhugo.com*
Hotline: *1- 888-778-0033*
Email: *info@miltonandhugo.com*

Ordering Information:
Quantity sales. Special discounts are granted to corporations, associations, and other organizations. For more information on these discounts, please reach out to the publisher using the contact information provided above.

Library of Congress Control Number:	2025901862
ISBN-13: 979-8-89285-418-4	[Paperback Edition]
979-8-89285-458-0	[Hardback Edition]
979-8-89285-419-1	[Digital Edition]

Rev. date: 01/30/2025

THE DECISION TO LEAVE

The decision to leave for Africa had not come easily, though it might have appeared that way to anyone on the outside. For M, the choice felt less like a decision and more like an inevitability—a desperate move by a man cornered by his own pain.

The weeks leading up to his departure were agonizing. Each day was a reminder of what he had lost: his children, his purpose, and any semblance of hope. The silence in his small apartment felt oppressive, the kind of quiet that didn't bring peace but rather amplified the storm in his mind. No amount of alcohol, no cocktail of substances could dull the ache in his chest.

When the idea struck him, it was as though the weight of his grief had forged it from sheer desperation. If his life was to end, it could at least mean something. The multimillion-dollar life insurance policy he'd taken out through Lloyd's of London felt like his last chance to provide for the daughter he could no longer see.

He shared his plan with only two people: his father and his best friend. His father, a man of few words but deep feelings, had struggled to hold back his tears when M explained what he intended to do. "You don't have to do this," his father said, his voice trembling. But M had made up his mind.

To everyone else, the story was simple: he had taken a six-month security contract in South Africa. It wasn't unusual for someone with his skills, and no one questioned it. But as M packed his few belongings, selling off everything else to tie up loose ends, the finality of his plan began to sink in.

THE FAREWELL

The morning of his departure was crisp and clear, the kind of day that felt cruel in its brightness. M's family gathered at the airport to see him off. His mother and sisters smiled, unaware of the true nature of his trip, while his father stood slightly apart, his expression betraying the sorrow he tried to hide.

"I'll see you in a few months," M lied, his voice steady despite the turmoil inside.

His younger sister hugged him tightly, her face lighting up with a smile. "You better," she teased.

M managed a chuckle, masking the thousand deaths he was dying inside. "I love you, sis," he said, his voice soft but sincere.

As he turned to walk toward the terminal, he forced himself to not look back. Each step felt heavier than the last, and by the time he reached the boarding gate, his heart felt like it was made of lead.

THE FLIGHT TO JOHANNESBURG

The flight was long, but M welcomed the solitude it offered. He leaned back in his seat, staring out the window as the world below faded into a blur of clouds. Sleep came sporadically, broken by flashes of memory and guilt.

He carried a leather-bound journal, a gift from his best friend who had insisted he take it with him. "Write everything down," his friend had said. "Even if no one else ever reads it, maybe it'll help you make sense of it all."

As the plane began its descent into Johannesburg, M pulled the journal from his bag and scribbled a few lines:

> *The pain is still there, but it feels...distant. Maybe it's the altitude. Or maybe I'm just too tired to feel it anymore.*

The wheels touched down with a jolt, and as the plane taxied to the gate, M closed the journal and prepared himself for the next phase of his journey.

ARRIVAL IN JOHANNESBURG

The first thing M noticed as he stepped out of the airport was the heat—a dry, relentless warmth that clung to his skin. The taxi ride into the heart of Johannesburg was a blur of sights and sounds. The city was a tapestry of contrasts, with gleaming skyscrapers towering over crowded markets and makeshift homes.

That night, he checked into the Bannister Hotel on De Beer Street, a modest but comfortable spot in the bustling city center. From his room on the top floor, he could see the Nelson Mandela Bridge illuminated against the night sky. The view was striking, but it did little to ease the turmoil inside him.

He spent the evening in the hotel bar, nursing a drink as he observed the locals and travelers who filled the space. The noise and laughter around him felt almost alien, a stark contrast to the heaviness he carried.

BOARDING THE BLUE TRAIN

The following morning, M made his way to Park Station, his destination now set: Cape Town. The Blue Train was legendary, known for its opulent first-class service and breathtaking views of South Africa's landscape. But M had chosen economy class, not out of frugality but because he wanted to stay grounded, to experience the journey as it truly was.

The economy cars were a world away from the polished luxury of first class. The air was thick and warm, the seats crammed with passengers of all ages. Vendors moved up and down the aisles, selling everything from warm beers to roasted peanuts, their voices blending into the hum of the train's engine.

M found a seat near the back of the carriage, next to a window. As the train pulled out of the station, he leaned against the glass.

THE BLUE TRAIN: A JOURNEY THROUGH SOUTH AFRICA

The morning was already sweltering at Park Station in Johannesburg, the bustling hub of South Africa's railway network. The platform buzzed with activity—hawkers shouting, passengers jostling, and the rhythmic clatter of trains pulling in and out. Amid the chaos, M boarded the Blue Train bound for Cape Town, a journey that promised to be as unpredictable as the landscape it traversed.

The economy-class carriage was packed filled with people of all ages and walks of life. Children clung to their mothers, wide-eyed and curious, while vendors shuffled through the narrow aisles, balancing trays of warm beers, roasted peanuts, and grilled meat. The air was thick and stifling, a mix of heat, sweat, and the aroma of spices from food shared among passengers. Despite the discomfort, there was an energy to the train—a raw vitality that mirrored the heartbeat of South Africa itself.

M settled into his seat near the back of the carriage, leaning against the window. Outside, the urban sprawl of Johannesburg began to fade, giving way to rolling hills dotted with small settlements and vast stretches of untamed wilderness. He watched the landscape unfurl like a painting, the golden grasses of the savanna blending seamlessly with jagged cliffs and distant mountain ranges.

For a while, M lost himself in the rhythm of the train, the steady *clack-clack* of the wheels against the tracks soothing the chaos in his mind. He spoke with a few locals, trading stories over warm beers bought from the vendors. Laughter and animated conversations filled the carriage, creating a sense of camaraderie that was hard to ignore.

THE SPARK OF CONFLICT

As the train sped farther into the countryside, M began to notice a growing tension in the air. It started subtly—a hushed exchange between two men at the far end of the carriage followed by sharp glances and muttered words. Soon, voices rose, and the uneasy harmony of the train shattered.

A heated argument had erupted between a group of white and black passengers. The shouting grew louder, with insults and slurs hurled back and forth. M, consumed by his own thoughts earlier, hadn't realized where he was seated until that moment. He was the only white man on the "black" end of the carriage—a distinction that carried weight he hadn't anticipated.

Suddenly, the argument turned to him. The white passengers at the other end of the car pointed at M, their voices laced with venom. "Verraaier!" they spat—traitor. At the same time, he could feel the eyes of the black passengers around him, their gazes wary, uncertain whether his presence was an act of solidarity or provocation.

M's pulse quickened, but his face remained calm. Instinctively, he reached down, tightening the laces on his boots. If a fight broke out, he was ready.

When the first punch was thrown, the chaos erupted in an instant. Fists flew, knives flashed, and the air filled with shouts and screams. M stayed seated, his imposing demeanor acting as a deterrent. While others clashed around him, no one dared challenge him directly.

The fight was brutal and quick, leaving several passengers injured and bleeding. The most seriously hurt were unceremoniously thrown off the train at the next stop. As the dust settled, the carriage slowly returned to an uneasy quiet, the remaining passengers nursing their wounds and avoiding each other's eyes.

A MOMENT OF UNDERSTANDING

M didn't move from his seat. He saw no reason to relocate to the "white" end of the train, despite the potential danger. This decision surprised the black passengers around him, sparking a ripple of conversation.

"Why didn't you leave?" an older man asked him, his voice tinged with both curiosity and suspicion.

M shrugged. "Why should I? I don't care about skin color. That's not why I'm here."

His words, simple but sincere, seemed to diffuse some of the lingering tension. Slowly, the passengers around him began to open up, sharing stories of their lives, their struggles, and their hopes.

One young man, barely out of his teens, spoke of his dream to become a doctor despite the barriers he faced. An elderly woman recounted her family's history, tracing it back to the days of apartheid. As they spoke, M listened, drawn into their world and momentarily forgetting his own pain.

The conversations lasted for hours, carrying the group through the rest of the journey. By the time the train neared Cape Town, M felt a strange connection to the people around him—a bond forged not by shared experiences, but by a mutual understanding of struggle and resilience.

THE ARRIVAL

As the Blue Train pulled into Cape Town station, the sun was setting, casting a warm, golden glow over the city. Table Mountain loomed in the distance, its flat peak shrouded in mist while the vibrant streets of Cape Town bustled with life.

M stepped off the train, his feet unsteady on the platform. He had no plan, no clear direction—only the weight of his purpose and the faint glimmer of something unexpected. The journey had been harrowing, yet it had also shown him a side of humanity he hadn't anticipated.

Looking back at the train now pulling away, M felt a pang of something he couldn't quite name. Hope? Regret? Perhaps both. For now, though, there was only the city before him and the path that lay ahead.

BIG BLUE: A GLIMPSE OF LIGHT IN THE DARKNESS

M arrived in Green Point, Cape Town, after a long day of wandering through the city. Exhaustion weighed heavily on him, but nothing he'd seen so far felt right. Just as he was about to give up for the night, he stumbled upon Big Blue Backpackers. The sight of the unassuming hostel, with its quirky blue exterior and inviting atmosphere, caught his eye. Something about it drew him in.

The moment he walked through the doors, M could feel the energy of the place. It was alive with laughter, music, and the mingling of accents from all over the world. Backpackers sat in the communal lounge, swapping stories, while others played pool or gathered around the outdoor braai, grilling food and chatting under the African night sky.

M booked a room, figuring he'd only stay a night or two, but Big Blue quickly became more than just a place to sleep—it became a haven.

In the mornings, the hostel came alive with the smell of freshly brewed coffee and sizzling eggs as the guests gathered in the communal kitchen. The breakfast table was a melting pot of cultures, with friends from every corner of the planet sharing meals and stories. There was Luca, the passionate Italian chef who insisted on teaching everyone how to make the perfect risotto; Nia, the free-spirited artist from New Zealand who spent her days painting murals on the hostel walls; and Ahmed, a soft-spoken Egyptian traveler who could tell captivating stories about his adventures in the Sahara.

For the first time in years, M felt accepted. There was no judgment, no need to hide the weight of his pain. These people, though strangers, treated him like family. Their warmth and camaraderie began to chip away at the walls he had built around himself.

FINDING CONNECTION

M had always been guarded, but something about the openness of the people at Big Blue made him let his guard down. Nights at the hostel were filled with conversations under the stars, debates about life and love, and shared dreams of far-off places. For once, M felt seen—not for his scars or his burdens, but for the person he was beneath it all.

One evening, as the group gathered around the fire pit, someone asked M about his story. Normally, he would have deflected or changed the subject; but that night, he found himself opening up. He didn't share everything, but he spoke of loss, of searching for meaning, and of his struggle to keep going.

"I came here looking for an ending," he admitted quietly, staring into the flickering flames.

His words hung in the air, but instead of pity or discomfort, there was only understanding. Nia reached out and placed a hand on his shoulder. "Maybe you'll find something else instead," she said softly.

A NEW KIND OF FAMILY

As the days turned into weeks, M realized he had found something he hadn't known he was searching for—a sense of belonging. The bonds he formed with the people at Big Blue were unlike anything he'd experienced before. They weren't just friendships, they were lifelines.

Each morning, they would cook breakfast together, laughing as they flipped pancakes or scrambled eggs. In the afternoons, they explored Cape Town, hiking up Lion's Head, visiting the markets at the V&A

Waterfront, or simply walking along the beach. Evenings were reserved for communal dinners and impromptu dance parties in the lounge.

These moments were simple, but they were transformative. For the first time in years, M felt alive—not because he was numbing his pain, but because he was experiencing joy.

A HARD LESSON

One night in Cape Town, M found himself at an open-air bar overlooking the vast, moonlit ocean. The salty breeze carried with it the chatter of patrons and the clinking of glasses, masking the tension simmering beneath the surface. M wasn't there for leisure. He was there on a mission—to infiltrate the criminal underworld and forge connections. He had spent months perfecting a backstory, crafting a persona rooted in his Irish heritage and fabricated ties to the IRA, knowing it could open the doors he needed.

As he sat nursing a beer at a weathered wooden table, he struck up a conversation with a group of men who seemed to fit the bill: hardened expressions, casual demeanor, and a way of carrying themselves that hinted at lives lived on the edge. They exuded the kind of confidence that M associated with seasoned criminals. Believing he'd finally found the right crowd, he began fishing for information, carefully dropping details from his rehearsed story to build credibility.

But unbeknownst to M, these men were not criminals—they were undercover operatives, part of an Interpol task force stationed in Cape Town. They were there for their own reasons, observing, listening, and probing for threats in the city's seedy underbelly.

The conversation started casually enough—shared beers, exchanged stories, and light banter—but M soon made a critical mistake. In his eagerness to impress and establish his cover, he broke the cardinal rule of undercover work: let the others do the talking. Instead, he began revealing too much, embellishing details of his fabricated past.

When he mentioned growing up in a small town in Northern Ireland, one of the men across the table—a rugged, sharp-eyed individual—stiffened slightly. The change was subtle but not lost on M. The man leaned forward, his voice steady but laced with suspicion.

"Really? What street did you grow up on?" the man asked, his tone deceptively casual.

M, confident in his preparation, rattled off a street name without hesitation. But the man's expression darkened immediately. "I lived on that street," he said, his voice now cold. "What house number?"

A cold chill ran down M's spine. The air seemed to thicken around him. He knew he had slipped, but he had no choice but to press on. He quickly supplied a house number, hoping to bluff his way through.

The man's eyes narrowed, and his lips curled into a grim smile. "I lived two houses down from there. You're full of shit—and you're lying." He leaned back slightly, his hand moving toward the waistband of his jeans. "You know what happens to liars like you?"

Time seemed to slow as the man drew a gun and pointed it directly at M's chest. Every instinct in M's body screamed at him to run, but there was nowhere to go. He was alone, outnumbered, and utterly exposed. With milliseconds to act, M's survival instincts kicked in fueled by adrenaline and desperation.

Instead of panicking, he reached for his beer, polished it off in a single gulp, and began to laugh—a low, confident chuckle that gradually grew louder. The tension at the table was palpable, and the other men stared at him, bewildered. Why was he laughing in the face of imminent death?

M locked eyes with the man holding the gun and smirked. "What makes you think I didn't want you to blow my cover? What makes you think this wasn't a test to vet *you*? How do you know I'm not already five steps ahead of you and your friends here?"

The man hesitated, his grip on the gun faltering ever so slightly. M leaned forward, his voice steady and deliberate. "How do you know I don't have a sniper on that rooftop across the street with his crosshairs right on your forehead? How do you know it's not you who's about to die tonight?"

The men exchanged uncertain glances, their initial confidence replaced by unease. Sensing he had the upper hand, M reached across the table, grabbed the man's beer, and downed it in one motion. Slamming the empty bottle back on the table, he leaned in closer. "Or maybe I'm just fucking with you. Or maybe I'm not."

The tension at the table reached a fever pitch, and for a moment, no one spoke. Then as if on cue, M burst into laughter, a deep belly laugh that echoed through the bar. The other men, caught off guard by the absurdity of the situation, began to laugh as well, though their laughter was tinged with uncertainty.

The man with the gun eventually chuckled and muttered, "Ah, fuck it. Let's drink." He holstered the weapon, and the group ordered another round of beers. For the next hour, they drank heavily, their initial tension dissolving into camaraderie. The men, now loose-lipped, revealed their true identities as Interpol operatives and shared details about their mission in Cape Town.

M played along, feigning drunkenness, but his mind was racing. He excused himself to use the restroom, his legs steady despite the alcohol he had consumed. Once out of sight, he made a hasty exit through the back door, his heart pounding in his chest. Outside, in the cool night air, his hands shook uncontrollably as the adrenaline coursed through his veins.

He had come perilously close to death or imprisonment that night. The lesson was clear: overconfidence could kill. He had underestimated his adversaries and let his guard down, but he had also learned the power of quick thinking and the value of composure under pressure. It was a night he would never forget—one that reinforced the dangerous stakes of the life he had chosen to lead.

A NIGHT ON LONG STREET

One humid summer night in Cape Town, M found himself lounging in the common area of Big Blue Backpackers, where travelers from all over the world gathered to share stories and plan adventures. Among them was Simon, a young German with a mischievous grin and a penchant for wild nights. With a beer in hand and a spark in his eyes, Simon leaned over and said, "Hey, you need to see Long Street. It's insane—clubs, bars, people everywhere. Come on, man, let's go have some fun."

M, needing a break from the relentless pressure of his current life, thought, *Why the hell not?* He hadn't let loose in a long time, and the idea of a carefree night was tempting. "All right," he said, finishing his drink, "let's do it."

The two set off, weaving through Cape Town's bustling streets as the city came alive with neon lights and pulsing music. Long Street was everything Simon had promised: a chaotic, intoxicating playground of packed bars, deafening music, and people spilling into the sidewalks. Simon and M dove into the night with reckless abandon, hopping from club to club, their inhibitions fading with every drink. The duo's laughter echoed as they danced, flirted, and toasted to the madness of the night.

Finally, they ended up at a multilevel dance club, its floors vibrating with bass-heavy beats. Simon led M to the second floor where a row of bathrooms overlooked the gyrating crowd below. Pulling M into one of the stalls, Simon grinned and produced a small bag of cocaine. "You in?" he asked.

M, caught up in the hedonistic whirlwind of the night, smirked and said, "Why the hell not?"

Simon quickly chopped out two fat lines on the bathroom counter, his movements hasty and practiced. Just as they leaned in, the pounding of fists on the bathroom door interrupted them. "Hurry up!" someone yelled from outside.

"Quick, do it all before they come!" Simon urged. They hurriedly snorted the lines, the rush hitting almost instantly, but just as they wiped the powder from their noses, the door burst open. Two massive bouncers stood there, flanked by a long line of irritated clubgoers. The bouncers' eyes locked on to M and Simon, their noses still dusted with telltale white residue.

"Out. Now," one of the bouncers growled, stepping forward.

But M wasn't about to go quietly. He threw all his weight into a shoulder-check, slamming into the first bouncer and sending him stumbling backward into the wall. Without missing a beat, M swung his elbow, connecting with the second bouncer's jaw in a sickening crunch. The man crumpled, clutching his face. In the chaos, Simon darted out of the stall, and M followed, the two of them sprinting down the stairs, weaving through the crowd as if their lives depended on it.

They burst out onto the street, adrenaline coursing through their veins, laughing like maniacs. Simon held up his hand, and M slapped it in a triumphant high-five. "That was insane!" Simon shouted over the noise of the street.

Still high and riding the thrill of their escape, M turned to Simon. "Wanna get more?"

Simon's grin widened. "Absolutely."

They climbed a steep side street, leaving the chaos of Long Street behind. Soon, they spotted a man leaning casually against a lamppost, his movements and furtive glances screaming *dealer*. Approaching him, Simon negotiated quickly, and the man handed over a small bag of cocaine in exchange for cash.

But M, too caught up in the moment, didn't notice the two police officers approaching from behind. "Hey! What's going on here?" one officer barked.

The dealer bolted, disappearing into the shadows. Simon froze, holding the bag like a deer in headlights, while M's heart dropped. One officer drew a baton, the other a pistol, their faces stern with no hint of humor. M knew how things worked here—bribery was often a solution, but these officers weren't biting.

One of the officers grabbed M's wrist. In that split second, M realized it was all or nothing. Without hesitation, he snatched the officer's gun, twisting it free with practiced precision, and slammed the butt of the weapon into the man's face. Blood sprayed as the officer crumpled. Before the second officer could react, M kicked his knee out, sending him sprawling onto the pavement.

M sprinted into the nearest alley, disassembling the firearm as he ran. The clinking of metal echoed as he threw the pieces in different directions, hoping to slow his pursuers. Behind him, the officers shouted in Afrikaans, their voices sharp and urgent. Sirens wailed in the distance, growing louder with every passing second.

Footsteps thundered behind him, but M didn't dare look back. He pushed himself harder, lungs burning, adrenaline overriding exhaustion. Suddenly, from a side alley, Simon appeared, tackling one of the pursuing officers like a linebacker. The officer hit the ground with a heavy thud, losing his baton in the process. Simon, grinning like a madman, scrambled to his feet and began running alongside M.

"This is fucking awesome!" Simon shouted, his voice breathless but exhilarated.

The two ran as if the devil himself were chasing them, darting through alleys and side streets until the sound of pursuit faded. Finally, they reached the familiar gates of Big Blue Backpackers. Stumbling into the courtyard, they collapsed onto the cool pavement, gasping for air.

For a moment, they lay there in silence, staring up at the night sky. Then the laughter started—wild, uncontrollable, and tinged with disbelief. The insanity of the night washed over them, and for the first time, M realized just how close he had come to disaster.

A QUIET BREAKDOWN

The courtyard of Big Blue Backpackers was usually a lively space filled with laughter, music, and the hum of conversation from travelers sharing stories of their adventures. But tonight, it was quiet. Most of the guests had retired for the evening, leaving M alone under the faint glow of a garden lantern.

He sat on a weathered chair tucked away in a secluded corner, hidden from view. The soft rustle of leaves and the distant hum of the city were the only sounds around him. The crushing weight of his pain bore down on him, relentless and unyielding. He clenched the arms of the chair, his knuckles white, as he fought to keep the tears at bay.

In this moment of vulnerability, M felt utterly alone, the darkness within him threatening to consume what little strength he had left. His thoughts spiraled, pulling him into the familiar abyss of regret, loss, and hopelessness. He whispered a silent prayer, not expecting an answer, just desperate to release the anguish clawing at his chest.

Then he felt it—a presence.

He didn't look up at first, unwilling to reveal his pain to anyone. The faint crunch of gravel underfoot reached his ears, and a figure emerged from the shadows. She moved quietly, almost delicately, as though sensing the fragility of the moment.

"Are you okay?"

Her voice, soft and laced with a German accent, broke through the suffocating silence. It wasn't just the words—it was the tone, tender and unintrusive, like a lifeline extended without expectation.

M's throat tightened, and he fought against the wave of emotion threatening to overwhelm him. He gave a slight nod, unable to trust his voice, hoping she would take it as a sign to leave. But she didn't.

Instead, she stepped closer and placed a gentle hand on his shoulder. The simple gesture startled him. It wasn't pity or awkward sympathy—it was something deeper, something he hadn't felt in a long time: genuine care.

"I don't think you're okay," she said, her voice unwavering but kind. "But whatever it is, I'm here for you."

That was all it took. The dam broke, and M's calloused heart cracked open. Sobs wracked his body as years of pain and grief poured out. He buried his face in his hands, trying to hide the tears, but there was no stopping them.

She didn't flinch or retreat. Instead, she knelt beside him, her presence steady and grounding. Her name, he would later learn, was Kimmy. As he cried, she reached up and gently placed her hands on either side of his face, tilting his head so their eyes met.

Her blue eyes, bright and vibrant, held no judgment, only empathy. They were a window into a soul so compassionate that M felt, for the first time in years, like he could let go of the weight he carried.

"Do you want to talk about it?" she asked, her voice as soothing as a lullaby.

M shook his head, unable to form words.

"That's okay," she said, her lips curving into a small smile. Without hesitation, she wrapped her arms around him in a hug so warm and sincere that it momentarily silenced the storm raging inside him.

M sat there, stunned by her kindness. He couldn't fathom how a stranger could care so deeply, how someone he had never met before could cut through his defenses with such ease.

AN INVITATION TO HOPE

After a while, M pulled himself together, wiping his face and sitting up straighter. "I think I'm going to bed," he said, his voice hoarse from emotion.

Kimmy stood, her movements graceful, but there were tears in her own eyes now. "Meet me at the front gate at 8:00 a.m.," she said firmly.

M hesitated. He wanted to decline, to retreat back into the safety of isolation, but there was something in her expression—an unspoken promise—that made him agree.

"Okay," he said reluctantly.

The next morning, M made his way to the front gate, unsure if she would even be there. But as he stepped outside, there she was. Kimmy stood bathed in the soft morning light, her golden hair catching the sun's rays and her blue eyes sparkling with excitement.

Beside her were two scooters. When she saw him, she broke into a radiant smile and ran up to him, wrapping him in a hug that left him momentarily speechless.

"I'm so glad you came," she said, her happiness contagious. "We're going on a road trip today. I want to show you something."

M felt a pang of self-consciousness, unsure why she was going out of her way for him. But Kimmy's enthusiasm was impossible to resist. Before he could protest, she handed him a helmet, climbed onto one of the scooters, and motioned for him to follow.

A JOURNEY OF HEALING

As they rode along the southern coast, the salty ocean breeze brushed against M's face, and the rhythmic hum of the scooter's engine was oddly soothing. Kimmy led the way, occasionally glancing back with a grin to make sure he was keeping up.

Their first stop was Clarence Drive, near Rooi-Els. The view took M's breath away—rugged cliffs cascading into the turquoise waters of the Atlantic, waves crashing against the rocks below. They stood together, the wind tugging at their clothes and hair as they gazed out over the endless horizon.

Kimmy turned to M, her voice soft but full of conviction. "See? There's so much beauty in the world if you just let yourself see it."

For a fleeting moment, M allowed himself to believe her.

They continued their journey, stopping at the African Penguin and Seabird Sanctuary in Gansbaai. The sight of the waddling penguins and the playful atmosphere made M laugh—a genuine, unguarded laugh that surprised even him. Kimmy teased him about his "penguin waddle," and for the first time in what felt like forever, M felt a sliver of joy.

Their final destination was Langezandt Fishermen's Village, a quaint and picturesque spot where they sat together on the beach, watching the sun dip below the horizon. As the sky turned shades of orange and pink, Kimmy leaned over, gently taking M's hand in hers.

"See?" she said softly. "I told you it would be okay."

In that moment, M felt something he hadn't in years—a sense of peace. Kimmy, with her unshakable kindness and warmth, had shown him a glimpse of a world he had long since forgotten.

THE FISHERMAN'S VILLAGE

As the afternoon sun began to dip lower in the sky, painting the horizon with golden hues, they arrived at Langezandt Fisherman's Village. The quaint seaside hamlet felt like a place untouched by time with its whitewashed cottages adorned with blue shutters, cobblestone paths winding through vibrant gardens, and the faint scent of saltwater carried on the breeze.

Kimmy led the way, her energy unwavering despite the long day of riding. "Come on," she called back to M, her voice light and musical. "You have to see the beach before the sun sets—it's magical."

They followed a narrow sandy path that opened onto the shoreline, where the sea stretched out endlessly before them. The beach was almost deserted, save for a few fishing boats anchored in the distance and the occasional seagull gliding overhead. The waves rolled in with a gentle rhythm, the sound blending harmoniously with the rustling of the wind through the dune grasses.

M paused for a moment, taking it all in. The scene was serene, almost surreal, as if they had stepped into a painting. The sky had begun its transformation, hues of orange and pink streaking across the heavens, their reflection shimmering on the water's surface.

Kimmy turned to him, her eyes sparkling with a joy that was infectious. "Isn't it beautiful?" she asked softly, her voice carrying an almost reverent tone.

M nodded, but words escaped him. Beautiful didn't feel like a strong enough word for what he was seeing—or what he was feeling.

A MOMENT OF VULNERABILITY

They found a spot on the sand and sat down, their scooters parked out of sight. Kimmy kicked off her shoes, digging her toes into the cool sand,

and leaned back on her hands, gazing out at the horizon. M sat beside her, quieter than usual, his gaze fixed on the rolling waves.

For a long time, neither of them spoke. The silence wasn't awkward; it was comfortable, the kind that only exists between two people who don't need to fill the air with empty words.

Finally, Kimmy broke the stillness. "You know," she began, her voice thoughtful, "there's something about this place that makes you feel… free. Like no matter what's weighing you down, it doesn't matter here. The ocean just takes it all away."

M didn't respond right away. He wanted to believe her, to let the waves carry away the crushing weight he had been holding on to for so long. But he wasn't sure if it was possible.

Kimmy seemed to sense his hesitation. She scooted closer, her shoulder brushing against his, and looked at him with an expression so tender it nearly broke him again. "Whatever you're carrying," she said gently, "it's okay to let it go. Even just for a little while."

M turned to her, the vulnerability in her words making him feel exposed but safe at the same time. He nodded slightly, not trusting himself to speak.

THE SUNSET

As the sun began to sink lower, casting the world in shades of amber and rose, Kimmy reached over and took M's hand. Her touch was soft, but there was a strength in it that steadied him. She didn't say anything; she didn't need to. Her presence alone was enough to remind him that he wasn't alone, at least not in this moment.

M stared at their intertwined hands, the simplicity of the gesture overwhelming him. It had been so long since he had felt truly connected to someone, and yet here was this stranger—this angel—who had stepped into his life with no reason to care, but cared anyway.

As the first stars began to emerge in the darkening sky, Kimmy turned to him, her blue eyes shimmering with sincerity. "See?" she said softly, her voice almost a whisper. "I told you it would be okay."

Her words struck something deep within him, a part of him he thought had been irreparably broken. At that moment, M realized that she wasn't just showing him a beautiful sunset or a picturesque village—she was showing him something far greater: the possibility of hope.

Overcome with emotion, M pulled her into a hug. It wasn't just a thank-you; it was an acknowledgment of everything she had given him in these few short days.

A NIGHT TO REMEMBER

As the night settled in, they made their way to a small whitewashed cottage near the beach. The interior was simple but charming, with a cozy fireplace and windows that framed the ocean like a living painting.

They spent the night talking, laughing, and sharing pieces of their lives. Kimmy's laughter was infectious, her joy filling the small cottage and banishing the shadows that had loomed over M for so long.

At one point, she taught him a German song, and though his accent was terrible, he sang along anyway, his off-key rendition sending Kimmy into fits of laughter. Tears streamed down her face, not from sadness but from pure, unfiltered joy.

M couldn't remember the last time he had laughed like that, the sound feeling foreign yet natural in his throat.

A NEW PERSPECTIVE

As the first light of dawn spread across the sky, the world seemed to slow down, caught in the tranquil silence of early morning. M and Kimmy sat together on the porch, the cool breeze from the ocean mingling with the warmth of the rising sun. The air was thick with the salty scent of the sea, and the sound of gentle waves crashing against the shore filled the space around them. Kimmy rested her head on M's shoulder, her presence as comforting and steady as the light spilling over the horizon.

The early morning was their moment—a fleeting slice of peace in a world that had often been too loud, too chaotic. Kimmy's voice broke the stillness, soft but firm. "You're going to be okay," she said, her words not just a reassurance but a statement of quiet certainty, as if she had already seen the truth in him that he had struggled to accept for so long.

M didn't answer immediately. He didn't need to. The weight of her words settled into him in a way he hadn't expected. For years, he had carried the burden of his past, the guilt, the loss, and the endless cycle of self-doubt. But now, as he sat there beside her, feeling her warmth and her unwavering belief, something inside him shifted. For the first time in a long while, he allowed himself to believe in the possibility that she was right—that despite all that had happened, he could still find a way to heal, to move forward.

The ride back to Big Blue was a blur. Time seemed to lose its grip on him as he drove, the landscape passing by like a dream. He was lost in thought, in the quiet reverie of his new understanding, his new perspective. He could feel the weight of his decisions, but somehow, it didn't feel as crushing as it once had. The days that followed were a blur as well, the hours slipping through his fingers like sand as he focused on moving his plan forward, taking each step with renewed purpose.

But the difference now was palpable. Gone was the sense of being fractured, of being lost in the fog of his own mind. He didn't feel broken anymore. He didn't feel empty. Something had shifted in him, and though the road ahead was still uncertain, there was a quiet strength within him now—a strength born from knowing that he wasn't facing it alone. Kimmy had seen him. She had seen past the scars, past the pain, to the person he truly was. And for the first time in years, he felt like he could face whatever lay ahead.

THE HARDEST GOODBYE

But like all good things, M knew his time at Big Blue would come to an end. The day of departure arrived sooner than he expected, and the realization hit him hard. That evening, the group gathered for one last supper. The table was filled with food, laughter, and tears as they celebrated the time they had shared.

"To family," Luca said, raising his glass.

"To family," they all echoed, clinking glasses as the reality of their impending separation settled over them.

M sat quietly, taking it all in. He hadn't expected to find anything in Cape Town, let alone a group of people who had made him feel whole again.

As the night wore on, Kimmy, the German angel who had taken a special place in his heart, lingered near him, her usual bright smile replaced by an expression of deep sadness. When the others began to drift off to their rooms, she finally spoke, her voice trembling.

"Do you really have to go?" she asked, her tears already welling up. "You don't have to do this. Stay, M. Please. Stay here. With us. With me."

Her words struck him harder than he expected. For a moment, he hesitated. Could he stay? Could this newfound sense of connection, the family he had found, and the promise of something more with Kimmy be enough to change his path?

But deep down, he knew his journey wasn't over. There was still a plan to carry out, and his purpose in Africa hadn't changed.

"I wish I could," M replied, his voice heavy with regret. "But I have to see this through. I owe it to myself—and to others."

Kimmy's tears began to fall freely as she struggled to find the words. "You don't have to do it alone," she said, her voice breaking. "You don't always have to be the one to carry everything on your shoulders."

M stepped closer and gently wiped a tear from her cheek. "Kimmy, you've shown me kindness I never thought I'd deserve. You made me feel…alive again. But this is something I have to do. I'm so sorry."

She tried to hold it together, but it was too much. Sobbing, she turned and ran back to her room at the backpackers, leaving M standing alone in the dim light of the courtyard.

He wanted to chase after her, to hold her one more time, to tell her that he wished things could be different. But he didn't. His path had already been set, and though his heart ached to stay and see what life could be like with Kimmy, he couldn't abandon his mission.

As he left Big Blue the next morning, his heart was heavier than ever. Yet in the midst of his pain, there was a glimmer of something he hadn't felt in a long time: hope. A hope that maybe, just maybe, once his journey was complete, he could find his way back to her. But for now, he walked away, leaving a piece of himself behind.

INTERNATIONAL BACKPACKERS: A NEW ALLY

After the emotional goodbyes in Cape Town, M returned to Johannesburg with a heavy heart and a renewed sense of determination. The train ride back was quieter this time, the conversations and camaraderie he had experienced on the journey south replaced by introspection and the growing weight of his plan.

Upon arriving in Johannesburg, M checked into the International Backpackers in Melville, a vibrant neighborhood known for its eclectic bars and artsy vibe. The hostel, often referred to as *home base* by travelers, was nestled among a row of quirky shops and cafes, its faded exterior hiding the bustling life within.

As M walked through the courtyard, he was struck by the lively energy of the place. Travelers from every corner of the world lounged by the pool, sipping drinks and swapping stories. The sound of laughter and faint music echoed from the common area. Despite his purpose, M felt a small sense of relief—at least here, the noise and activity might drown out his thoughts for a while.

He was assigned a bed in one of the shared dorm rooms at the back of the hostel. The space was modest but functional, with bunk beds lining the walls and well-worn backpacks piled in corners. As he stepped into the room, he noticed another man unpacking his belongings on the opposite side.

The man was tall, broad-shouldered, and carried himself with the unmistakable air of someone who had seen combat. His scruffy beard and weathered appearance suggested he wasn't just another carefree traveler. M's instincts kicked in immediately—this guy was military, no doubt about it.

Before M could say anything, the man turned and extended a hand. "E," he said, his voice steady and confident.

M shook his hand, nodding slightly. "M."

E's eyes flicked to the tattoo on M's neck, a design only someone with specific military knowledge would recognize. He tilted his head, intrigued. "SWCC? You a boat guy?"

M hesitated for a moment before replying. "Sorta."

That simple exchange was enough to break the ice. Over the next few minutes, the two men fell into an easy conversation, their shared backgrounds creating an unspoken bond. E revealed that he was a former Army Ranger with Second Battalion, a seasoned operator who had seen his fair share of action. He mentioned that he'd recently been approached by the CIA for a field operator position but had turned it down.

"I've had enough of the government's games," E said, his tone laced with a mix of frustration and defiance. "I'm here to start something for myself. Diamonds, actually. Got some orders lined up for the new diamond exchange."

M couldn't help but respect the man's drive. There was a quiet intensity to E, a determination that mirrored his own. Feeling a rare sense of trust, M decided to open up about his own reason for being in Africa.

He told E about the life insurance policy, his plan to fake his death, and his hopes of securing financial stability for his daughter. As the words spilled out, M didn't sugarcoat the grim reality of what he intended to do. "I don't plan on making it out of this alive," he admitted.

E leaned back, sipping his beer as he processed M's story. There was no judgment in his expression, only a flicker of something M couldn't quite place—admiration, perhaps, or maybe just a deep understanding of what it meant to be broken.

"Damn, dog," E said finally. "That's heavy. But you know what? Sounds like the kind of adventure I can't pass up. Mind if I tag along?"

M raised an eyebrow. "You want in on this? You know how it ends, right?"

E shrugged, a sly grin spreading across his face. "I like a challenge. And besides, if we're gonna do this, might as well do it right."

A PLAN IN MOTION

That night, the two men sat by the pool, their beers sweating in the humid Johannesburg air as they hashed out a plan. E's experience as a Ranger brought a level of precision and strategy that M hadn't anticipated. Together, they mapped out the logistics, combining their knowledge to create a blueprint for the next phase of M's mission.

Their conversation ranged from the practical to the absurd punctuated by moments of dark humor that only two men who had lived through hell could appreciate. By the end of the night, M felt something he hadn't in a long time—hope.

For the first time since arriving in Africa, he wasn't facing his journey alone. E's presence, his unwavering confidence, and his willingness to dive headfirst into the unknown gave M a sense of reassurance. The partnership felt natural, as if fate had brought them together for a purpose neither fully understood yet.

BROTHERHOOD IN THE MAKING

Over the next few days, M and E became inseparable. They explored the streets of Melville together, blending in with the eclectic crowd at local cafes and bars. At the hostel, they earned the respect of fellow travelers, their stories of past exploits captivating everyone who listened.

E had a knack for making people laugh, his sharp wit and fearless attitude a stark contrast to M's quiet intensity. Yet the two balanced each other perfectly—E's boldness pushed M to step out of his comfort zone while M's measured approach kept E grounded.

Their bond deepened as they trained together, running drills and preparing for the dangers ahead. E's Ranger training brought a level of discipline and focus that M hadn't realized he needed. And in return, M shared his own hard-earned knowledge, their mutual respect growing with each passing day.

It wasn't long before their partnership began to feel less like a tactical alliance and more like a brotherhood. Both men had been broken in their own ways, their scars—visible and invisible—binding them together in a way few others could understand.

As they finalized their plan, neither could have predicted just how much their loyalty and friendship would be tested.

A WILD ROUTINE

Every morning, E and M would wake up at the crack of dawn, shaking off the haze of the previous night. Their days began the same way—piling into their tiny, beat-up compact rental car, the kind of vehicle that looked like it had already lived a full life before it ended up in their hands.

Without fail, E would slam Andrew W.K.'s "Party Hard" through the car speakers, cranking the volume to its absolute limit. The bass rattled the cheap plastic interior, and the music became their anthem—a raw, rebellious soundtrack to their chaotic mission. They'd tear through the streets of Johannesburg, laughing like madmen as E, behind the wheel, sought out the city's infamous speed bumps.

"Hold on!" E would yell, grinning like a kid as he floored the accelerator. The little rental car would hit the bump at full speed, launching into the air for a fleeting, exhilarating moment of weightlessness before slamming back onto the asphalt.

"YES!" they'd scream in unison, the adrenaline coursing through their veins. For those few moments, their burdens seemed lighter, their laughter echoing through the cramped car.

It wasn't the most discreet way to travel, but for E and M, it felt like freedom—a brief escape from the grim task they had set out to accomplish.

THE SEARCH FOR THE SHADOW ORGANIZATION

Over the next few days, they scoured the city, digging into the murky underworld of Johannesburg. They frequented shady bars, dingy cafes, and back-alley spots where whispers of illegal dealings hung in the air like cigarette smoke. Their goal was clear: find the elusive organization rumored to be the masterminds of elaborate life insurance fraud schemes.

The stories they uncovered painted a picture of an operation so skilled it bordered on myth. This group was said to have successfully extracted and relocated members of the French Foreign Legion—an almost impossible feat. The legion was notorious for hunting down deserters with ruthless precision, deploying highly trained operatives to track their targets across the globe.

"If these guys can outmaneuver the legion," E had said one evening, leaning back in his chair with a smirk, "they might be just crazy enough to help us."

M nodded, his mind racing with possibilities. It was a long shot, but it was their best shot. Still, they knew they couldn't just walk up to the organization empty-handed—they needed leverage. Something valuable. Something that would make them impossible to ignore.

THE GHOST

After hours of debate and planning, they settled on a plan. The word on the street was that an ex-KGB operative, known only as the Ghost, was operating in the region under a forged Bosnian identity. He was a middleman for the Triads, funneling automatic weapons and military-grade equipment into Southern Africa by the conex load. This wasn't small-time smuggling; this was large-scale arms dealing on an industrial level.

E scoffed at the name when they first heard it. "The Ghost? That's what they're going with? Sounds like something out of a bad spy novel."

M chuckled. "Yeah, but apparently, this guy lives up to it. He's been avoiding capture for years. No one's even seen his face."

The kicker? The Ghost was reportedly the archnemesis of the very organization E and M were trying to infiltrate. If they could deliver him—or at least disrupt his operation—they'd have the ultimate bargaining chip.

But catching the Ghost wasn't going to be easy. He was a man of shadows, someone who had evaded authorities, rival gangs, and international agencies alike. His network was tight, his operations seamless, and his reputation as a phantom unshakable.

FORGING A PLAN

Sitting in a dimly lit room with a map spread across the table, E and M laid out their strategy. Years of combat and operational experience had sharpened their instincts, and their respective military backgrounds gave them the kind of edge you couldn't teach.

"He's got to be moving through major ports," M said, tracing the map with his finger. "Durban, Cape Town maybe. But he's smart. He'll avoid high-profile routes."

E nodded. "Which means he's probably relying on smaller operations to distribute locally. We hit those, we rattle the cage, and see if we can flush him out."

"We're going to need intel," M added. "And a lot of it. People like this don't slip unless you make them."

E grinned, his confidence unshakable. "That's where we come in. If this guy's good, we'll have to be better. Time to turn up the heat."

The plan was risky, bordering on reckless, but that was exactly how E and M operated. The stakes were high, but so was the potential payoff.

For them, it wasn't just about getting the organization's attention—it was about proving they were willing to go to the ends of the earth to see their plan through.

And if the Ghost was everything the rumors claimed he was, it would take every ounce of their training, cunning, and determination to bring him down.

THE PLAN TO FIND THE GHOST

M and E knew that moving the sheer volume of military-grade weaponry attributed to the Ghost required more than just cunning—it demanded systemic protection. The logistics alone were staggering, involving vast quantities of firearms, ammunition, and equipment regularly crossing borders or moving within the country. There was no way such an operation could function without someone high up in law enforcement providing cover.

Over late-night strategy sessions, they hypothesized how this might work. South Africa's firearm regulations, though strict, had a peculiar loophole: the collector's license. Such a license allowed individuals to own a wide range of weaponry, from vintage firearms to military-grade assault rifles, so long as they were ostensibly for "collector" purposes.

"Perfect cover," M mused, leaning back in his chair. "If you can get a collector's license, you can mask just about any kind of weapons trafficking operation as long as no one looks too closely."

E nodded, thoughtfully sipping his beer. "And the Ghost? He's supposed to be a fanatical collector, right? That would explain how he's stayed under the radar for so long. No one questions it because it looks legitimate."

From there, they worked their network of informants, talking to every criminal and shady contact they could find. The process was slow and often frustrating, but their persistence paid off. After days of digging, they narrowed the Ghost's potential location to a single zip code—a district known for its mix of affluent estates and tightly controlled access.

"That's where he's operating," E said, tapping the map. "But we need proof. He's got to be registered with the local precinct as a collector if he's moving that much hardware. That's our way in."

CRAFTING THE COVER

The plan they devised was risky but clever. They would pose as representatives of wealthy American gun collectors searching for an elusive weapon: the Mauser C96 "Broomhandle" Red 9. The choice wasn't random—word on the street was that the Ghost had a passion for Mauser pistols, supposedly owning hundreds of them. Yet despite his infamous reputation, no one had ever seen his collection firsthand.

"That'll pique his interest if it gets back to him," M said.

"And even if it doesn't, the story will give us access to his records," E added, smirking.

The two spent hours rehearsing their cover story, ironing out every detail until it was airtight. By the time they were ready, they could talk convincingly about Mausers, obscure gun history, and wealthy collectors back in the States.

INFILTRATING THE PRECINCT

The local police station was an imposing structure, a three-story fortress surrounded by a high wall and guarded by armed officers. As M and E strolled through the gates, their eyes took in every detail: the armored technical vehicles parked in the lot, the heavy weaponry staged near the entrances, and the clusters of officers milling about.

"This is some crazy shit," M muttered under his breath, glancing at E.

E chuckled. "I know, right? Just keep your cool."

Inside, the tension was palpable. The station bustled with activity, and the air smelled faintly of coffee and sweat. The two men walked with the casual confidence of seasoned professionals, carrying themselves as though they belonged. At the reception desk, they politely requested a meeting with the police captain, explaining they were on a mission to locate a rare collector's item.

The receptionist raised an eyebrow but picked up the phone. A few minutes later, they were escorted through multiple security checkpoints, their senses on high alert. Every corridor, every doorway, every glance from the officers they passed was carefully cataloged. They mapped out potential escape routes in their minds, planning for worst-case scenarios.

Finally, they reached the captain's office on the top floor. The room was spacious but utilitarian, its most prominent feature a wall lined with filing cabinets and a large framed photo of the captain standing triumphantly over a lion during a safari hunt.

The captain, a stocky man with a sharp gaze, welcomed them in. "What can I do for you, gentlemen?"

M and E launched into their cover story, speaking with practiced ease about their "wealthy clients" and their hunt for the elusive Mauser Red 9. The captain listened with mild interest, occasionally nodding as he leaned back in his chair.

When they inquired whether he knew of any local collectors who might have such a piece, the captain straightened and opened a ledger book from his desk. As he flipped through the pages, M and E exchanged a quick glance—this was exactly what they had hoped for.

THE CRITICAL MOMENT

"Yes," the captain said, stopping on a page. "I believe there is someone in my district who could help you, but he is very private. A true collector. I doubt he'd want visitors."

As he spoke, his fingers hovered over the open ledger, tracing the lines on the page. M's sharp eyes flicked to the book, memorizing as much as he could in the brief moments the ledger was visible. It wasn't enough—he needed more.

Thinking fast, M pointed to the large photograph on the wall behind the captain. "That's quite the lion," he said, injecting a tone of admiration into his voice. "You must have a hell of a story to go with that picture."

The captain's face lit up, his pride evident. "Oh, that hunt was one of the greatest experiences of my life," he said, standing up and walking toward the photo. "It was taken in the Limpopo province. Took us three days to track that beast."

As the captain launched into a detailed account of his safari, M turned slightly, his body language relaxed, keeping the captain's attention focused on the photo. E, meanwhile, moved with practiced subtlety. As soon as the captain's back was turned, he slid closer to the desk, pulling his phone from his pocket.

With a quick glance to ensure the coast was clear, E snapped a photo of the open page in the ledger, the faint *click* of the phone's camera muffled by the captain's booming voice recounting the final moments of the hunt.

PLAYING IT COOL

E slipped back to his seat as the captain turned, his story winding down. "Quite the trophy," M said, nodding appreciatively. "You must have nerves of steel to face something like that."

The captain chuckled, clearly enjoying the flattery. "It's all about patience and precision," he said, settling back into his chair.

"Well, we appreciate your help," M said, smoothly steering the conversation back to their cover story. "We completely understand if this collector prefers his privacy. We'll see if we can explore other avenues for sourcing the Red 9."

The captain seemed satisfied with this response. "It's always tricky with collectors," he said. "But best of luck in your search."

The two men thanked him, shaking his hand before making their way back through the labyrinth of hallways and security checkpoints. Every step felt heavier with the weight of what they had just pulled off.

THE WALK BACK

As they exited the police station, the late-afternoon sun was glaring, casting long shadows across the parking lot. The armored vehicles and heavily armed officers seemed even more imposing in the bright light.

"Think he had any idea?" M asked under his breath as they crossed the lot.

E smirked. "Not a clue. But damn, that was close."

THE ESCAPE AND REALIZATION

M and E walked out of the police station, their pace measured, their faces unreadable. The information they had obtained felt like a victory, but the air around them was charged with tension. As soon as they reached their car, E slid into the driver's seat, pulling out his phone to double-check the photo of the ledger.

M stared at him as E's expression darkened. "We don't have much time," E muttered.

"What do you mean?" M asked.

E glanced at him. "Think about it. That police captain's no fool. If he's in this guy's pocket, the first thing he'll do after we leave is make a call. He'll warn the Ghost that someone's been asking questions."

M's jaw tightened. "So, what do we do?"

E didn't hesitate. "We go now. Straight to the address. If we wait, we lose our chance."

M nodded, adrenaline already coursing through his veins. E threw the car into gear, and they sped off, navigating the busy streets of Johannesburg with purpose.

THE STAKEOUT

They arrived at the location a little over half an hour later, parking discreetly down the street. The house was nondescript, a modest property at the end of a quiet cul-de-sac, but it had one distinct feature: a walk-out garage door in the basement partially concealed by the slope of the hill.

The two sat in the car, tension thick between them as they observed the property. "You think he's home?" M asked, his voice low.

E shrugged, his sharp eyes scanning the surroundings. "Doesn't matter. If this is him, he's not the kind of guy who just leaves loose ends lying around. We have to move before he does."

Minutes ticked by, the waiting stretching their nerves taut. Suddenly, they saw movement at the top of the hill. A man dressed in a garbage collector's uniform was walking toward the house.

E's gaze narrowed. "That's him, isn't it?"

M nodded, his breath catching as he noticed the man's hand—or rather, the absence of three fingers. The sight confirmed the street legend: the Ghost, known for his twisted, almost ritualistic violence, had once lost a fight to an enraged baboon while engaging in one of his grotesque "games."

The story had spread like wildfire through the criminal underworld. The Ghost reportedly tracked down baboons with newborns, murdering the babies in front of the mothers to provoke a fit of primal rage. Then he'd fight the mother baboon in hand-to-hand combat, testing his strength against the animal's ferocity.

The story was horrifying enough, but the missing fingers added an unsettling layer of truth to it. "That's him," M said quietly, his voice filled with certainty.

E smirked. "Well, no turning back now."

M opened the car door and stepped out, his movements calm and deliberate. "If I'm not back in twenty minutes," he said over his shoulder, "I'm dead."

E nodded, his expression unreadable. "Good luck," he said, gripping the wheel tightly as M slammed the door shut.

THE APPROACH

As M walked toward the man, his pulse pounded in his ears, but his exterior remained calm. He called out as he closed the distance, forcing a friendly tone into his voice.

"Hey there! How's your day going?"

The Ghost stopped in his tracks, turning to face M with an expression of mild suspicion. Up close, the man's presence was even more intimidating.

His face was weathered, his posture tense yet controlled, like a predator assessing its prey.

"Who's asking?" the Ghost replied, his accent betraying faint traces of Eastern Europe, though it was masked by years of living under a false Bosnian identity.

M smiled, keeping his hands visible and his demeanor non-threatening. "Just a guy with a lot of questions—and maybe some answers you'll want to hear."

The Ghost tilted his head, his eyes narrowing. The missing fingers on his hand flexed involuntarily, as if remembering the fight that had taken them. "I don't have time for games," he said, his voice low and dangerous.

"Neither do I," M replied, his tone hardening slightly. "But I think you'll want to hear what I have to say."

The Ghost hesitated for a moment, his sharp gaze scanning M for any sign of deceit. Finally, he nodded toward the garage door. "Follow me," he said curtly.

M felt a jolt of adrenaline as he followed the Ghost down the driveway to the walk-out garage. His eyes darted around, cataloging every detail—the faded paint on the door, the security camera tucked discreetly under the eaves, the heavy padlock on the side gate.

The Ghost unlocked the garage door and stepped inside "So," the Ghost said, turning to face M. "What do you want?"

M swallowed hard, keeping his composure. "I've got a proposition," he began, his voice steady. "One that could be mutually beneficial."

INTO THE LAIR

The Ghost gestured for M to follow him through the garage, his steps deliberate and his demeanor coldly commanding.

Then M saw it: a ship bulkhead door molded seamlessly into the concrete wall. It was completely out of place in the modest, unassuming house above them, and its sheer industrial nature hinted at something far more sinister below.

The Ghost stepped forward, gripping the massive wheel in the center of the door and spinning it with practiced ease. The sound of steel locking bars sliding echoed through the space, a mechanical growl that seemed to reverberate in M's chest. As the door swung open, M felt the air grow heavier, as if he were descending into another world.

Inside, the first room was a gunsmithing workshop, complete with meticulously arranged tools, half-assembled firearms, and bins of parts. The Ghost didn't stop there though. At the back of the workshop stood another bulkhead door, just as imposing as the first.

M's pulse quickened as the Ghost spun the locking mechanism again. The second room revealed itself to be an armory lined with crates of ammunition and shelves stacked with explosives of all types. The sheer volume was staggering, far beyond what even the boldest arms dealer might keep on hand. But the Ghost wasn't finished.

At the back of the armory was yet another bulkhead door. M couldn't help but marvel at the scale of the operation—the rooms were massive, far larger than the modest house above suggested. As the final door swung open, M stepped inside and froze.

THE HEART OF THE COLLECTION

The last room was unlike anything M had ever seen. Crates and crates of weapons, both military grade and antique, were stacked neatly around the space. Display tables stood in the center, each one laid out with an arsenal that spanned decades of warfare: assault rifles, sniper rifles, submachine guns, and handguns. Every weapon imaginable was present, polished to perfection.

But it was the back wall that truly stole M's breath. A massive pegboard stretched across the wall lined with close to 150 Mauser Broomhandle pistols. Each one was displayed like a piece of fine art, with twenty of them bearing the iconic red "9" of the Mauser C96 Red 9. The Ghost stepped forward, his movements slow and deliberate, his hand brushing over the Mausers with an air of reverence.

"These," he said quietly, almost to himself, "are my pride and joy."

M tried to keep his composure, his mind racing. This was it—the Ghost had bought the story so far, but the next few moments would determine everything.

THE TEST

As M began to explain his "collector's interest" and pitch the story, the Ghost's sharp gaze never left him. The man's skepticism was palpable, a predator's instinct sniffing out prey. M knew he was on thin ice.

Midway through the conversation, the Ghost suddenly pointed to an antique rifle mounted on the wall, his expression unreadable. "What caliber is that?" he asked, his tone deceptively casual.

M felt a chill run down his spine. He had no idea. Despite his rehearsed lines and surface-level knowledge of antique weapons, he hadn't studied enough to identify the rifle. His mind scrambled for a response, knowing hesitation could cost him his life.

The Ghost's hand twitched toward the back of his waistband, where the outline of a concealed firearm was visible. M's heart raced. He was too far to disarm the man, too exposed to make a move. He had seconds to act.

Without missing a beat, M pointed to an HK G36 assault rifle hanging on another wall and said confidently, "I'll be honest—I don't know much about that old gun. But I'm more of a fan of modern weapons like the G36." He added with a slight smirk, "Although I don't love the amount of distance between the barrel and the rail system. I prefer it closer for better accuracy."

The Ghost paused, his hand relaxing slightly. His lips curled into a faint smile, the tension in the room easing just enough for M to breathe.

"You've got an eye for detail," the Ghost said, his voice taking on a more approving tone.

THE SALE

The Ghost shifted his focus back to the pegboard, gesturing toward the Mausers. "Now, let me show you what a *real* collector cares about," he said, his pride evident.

He launched into a detailed explanation of his collection, pointing out the rarest pieces and their unique features. M nodded along, making appreciative comments and subtly steering the conversation back to his fabricated mission.

As they haggled over prices and the number of Mausers his "collectors" in the States would like to purchase, M's nerves began to settle. The Ghost seemed to have fully bought into the story, his initial suspicion replaced by the excitement of discussing his prized collection.

E WAITS

Meanwhile, outside in the car, E sat with the engine idling, his fingers drumming against the steering wheel. He glanced at the clock, his jaw tightening as the minutes stretched on.

"You've got this, M," he muttered to himself, his eyes fixed on the garage.

Despite his confidence in M's abilities, E couldn't shake the uneasy feeling in his gut. If anything went wrong, there was little he could do from the car. The Ghost wasn't the kind of man you could bluff twice.

THE WAY OUT

Back inside, M finalized the terms of the deal, carefully navigating the conversation to avoid raising any more suspicion. He made a point of expressing admiration for the Ghost's collection, throwing in just enough technical knowledge to keep the illusion intact.

"Well," M said eventually, glancing at his watch, "I'd better not keep my associate waiting. I'll relay the details to the collectors, and we'll be in touch."

The Ghost nodded, his demeanor calm but unreadable. "You know how to find me," he said, his tone carrying a subtle warning.

M extended his hand, which the Ghost shook firmly.

A TENSE INTRODUCTION

As M and the Ghost emerged from the labyrinthine garage back into the driveway, the late afternoon sun had dipped lower, casting long shadows across the hill. The heavy steel door of the garage clanged shut behind them, sealing the Ghost's world of secrets once more.

It had been exactly twenty-three minutes. The Ghost's sharp eyes immediately locked on to E, who sat behind the wheel of the car at the top of the hill, his figure outlined in the windshield.

"That's your buddy, isn't it?" the Ghost asked, his voice low and measured.

M's pulse quickened, but he kept his demeanor calm. "Yeah, that's him," he replied evenly.

The Ghost smirked faintly, his hand resting casually on his hip—a movement that, to M, felt deliberate, a subtle reminder of the concealed weapon he carried. "Why don't you have him come down here? I'd like to meet him."

M turned slightly and motioned to E, who hesitated for a moment before stepping out of the car. His movements were deliberate but cautious as he made his way down the hill to the driveway. M could feel the tension radiating off his friend, though E masked it well behind a practiced, relaxed posture.

As E approached, the Ghost's gaze lingered on him, assessing him with the same predator-like intensity he'd shown M earlier. "So, you're the one backing him up," the Ghost said, his tone neither friendly nor hostile—just a statement, as though he were cataloging a new piece of information.

E nodded, extending his hand. "That's right. E. Good to meet you."

The Ghost's grip was firm as he shook E's hand, his eyes never leaving his. "So, you're into Mausers too?"

E grinned slightly, his confidence kicking in. "I've got a collector's eye for detail, but M's the real enthusiast. I'm just here to make sure the right deals get made."

The Ghost studied him for a moment longer before finally nodding. The tension in the air eased slightly as the three fell into a brief but measured conversation. The Ghost seemed satisfied with their story, and the deal was finalized: M and E would be back soon with their "client's" terms.

"Pleasure doing business," the Ghost said, a hint of finality in his voice.

THE CELEBRATION

As M and E climbed back into the rental car, they held their composure until they rounded the first corner out of sight. Then, as if on cue, they exploded into shouts of celebration.

"YES! We fucking did it!" M yelled, punching the air as E reached over to slap his hand in a high five.

E laughed, his voice filled with equal parts disbelief and exhilaration. "Man, I can't believe that just happened. We found the Ghost! And he bought the whole damn thing!"

M leaned back in his seat, letting out a breath he hadn't realized he'd been holding. "And I almost fucking died," he added with a grin, recounting the tense moment in the armory when the Ghost had questioned him about the antique rifle.

E's jaw dropped as he listened. "Are you serious? He almost pulled on you?"

"Damn right he did," M said, shaking his head. "I had no clue what the hell that rifle was. Had to bluff my ass off and talk about the HK G36 instead. Thank God he bought it."

E shook his head in disbelief. "Man, that's some James Bond–level shit right there. You kept your cool like a pro."

M laughed, the tension finally breaking into pure exhilaration. "No one's ever going to believe this, you know. Hell, I can hardly believe it myself."

E grinned, slamming his foot on the accelerator as the little car roared (or sputtered) down the street. "This calls for a celebratory song!"

Reaching for the stereo, E blasted their anthem—Andrew W.K.'s "Party Hard"—as they both yelled along to the lyrics, pounding the dashboard in rhythm. The car bounced slightly over a speed bump, but instead of cursing, they burst into another round of laughter.

"Man, this is insane!" E shouted over the music. "We just walked into the lair of the most dangerous guy in South Africa, and we walked out with a deal. Who the hell are we right now?"

M smirked. "We're the guys who just pulled off the impossible."

"Damn right we are," E said, gripping the wheel tightly. "Now, let's figure out how to use this against him before he realizes he might've made a mistake."

As they sped down the road, the adrenaline of the moment fueled their laughter and shouts. They both knew the celebration was temporary—the real challenge was still ahead. But for now, they allowed themselves this small victory, savoring the surreal reality of what they'd just accomplished.

E glanced at M with a grin. "You know," he said, his tone light but thoughtful, "this feels like something straight out of a movie. Like, if we ever told anyone, they'd just laugh in our faces."

M chuckled, leaning back in his seat. "Yeah. Good thing we're the only ones who'll ever know."

The two fell into a comfortable silence, the pounding music still filling the car. Despite the chaos and danger they'd just navigated, they were alive—and, for the moment, they were untouchable.

AN UNEXPECTED VISITOR

That night, back at International Backpackers, M and E were still riding the high of their recent victory with the ghost, celebrating over a few well-earned drinks. The tension of the past weeks had momentarily eased, and the two friends were enjoying the camaraderie that came with triumph. But the night took an unexpected turn when M's phone buzzed.

It was Kimmy.

His heart skipped a beat as he answered, and her voice, soft but trembling with emotion, came through the line. She was in Johannesburg. Not just anywhere in Johannesburg—she was in Melville. She had traveled all this way, across the entire country, in search of him. She wanted to see him one last time.

M could hardly believe it. E, overhearing the conversation, raised an eyebrow, his usual skepticism kicking in. "A girl traveled across the country and spent two days wandering through Jo'burg looking for you? Sounds like a movie plot," he teased. But despite his doubts, E was up for an adventure, so the boys laced up their boots and headed out to meet her at a local bar.

When M saw her, his breath caught in his throat. Kimmy spotted him first and ran toward him, throwing her arms around him as tears welled up in her eyes. "I'm so glad I found you," she whispered, her voice thick with emotion.

M felt a wave of emotion crash over him like a tidal wave. Disbelief, joy, guilt, and sorrow all battled for dominance in his mind. He couldn't understand how she could care for him so deeply—to leave the comfort of her world to search for him in a place as chaotic and dangerous as Johannesburg.

As they sat at the end of the bar, just a few feet from E, Kimmy poured out her heart. She begged him to come back to Germany with her, to leave everything behind and start a life together. Her voice quivered with desperation, and M could see the belief in her eyes—the belief that he didn't have to follow through with his plan, that they could leave the chaos behind and forge something beautiful together.

M wanted to say yes. He wanted it more than anything. But the weight of his mission bore down on him like a millstone around his neck. So much effort, sacrifice, and planning had gone into this unfolding operation. He felt obligated—no, destined—to see it through, no matter the cost.

He tried to explain, updating her on what they had accomplished so far, attempting to reassure her that if he survived, if he made it through this alive, he would find her, and they could build the life she dreamed of. But the words felt hollow even as he spoke them. Kimmy, unconvinced, clung to his hand, tears streaming down her face.

"Please, M," she pleaded. "You don't have to do this. You've done enough. Come with me. Please."

Her words tugged at something deep within him—the tender, soft side of his heart that yearned for peace, for love, for a life away from the constant storm. But alongside it flickered another part of him—the hardened, calloused side forged through years of struggle and pain.

For a moment, the softer side almost won. He could see it: the two of them, together, building a new life far away from the chaos. He wanted it so badly that it hurt.

But then the switch flipped.

The calloused side took over, and in a voice devoid of the warmth he truly felt, he told her goodbye. Kimmy's sobs filled the air as she clung to him, but M gently pulled away.

"I'm sorry," he said, his voice cold despite the anguish in his chest. "But I have to do this."

Kimmy collapsed back into her seat at the bar, tears streaming down her face, her shoulders shaking with the weight of her heartbreak. M turned and walked toward the door, E following silently behind him.

As the door swung shut behind them, the night air hit M like a slap in the face. He didn't look back, but the image of Kimmy, sitting there broken and alone burned itself into his memory.

Regret gnawed at him, even as he forced himself to focus on the mission ahead. Years later, he would look back on that night and wonder if he had made the right choice. He had told himself it was for the greater good, but in his heart, he knew that he had left behind something rare, something precious—something he would never find again.

As M and E turned to leave the bar, the weight of the moment hung heavy in the air. Kimmy's quiet sobs echoed behind them, a heart-wrenching soundtrack to their departure. M forced himself to keep walking, his shoulders stiff with the effort of not looking back, his mind a chaotic storm of emotions.

E followed close behind, his usual stoic demeanor intact—but as they neared the door, a faint expression of sadness flickered across his rugged face. It was subtle, barely perceptible, but it was there: a crack in his tough exterior.

E had seen his share of heartbreak, had witnessed countless goodbyes in the relentless tide of their lives. Yet something about Kimmy's raw, unguarded sorrow struck a chord deep within him. He didn't say anything, but his silence spoke volumes.

M caught the shift in E's expression out of the corner of his eye, and it only deepened the ache in his chest. For all his hardened resolve, for all his determination to follow through with the mission, seeing E—his steadfast, unshakable friend—show even a hint of sadness almost undid him.

As they stepped out into the cool night air, M's mind churned with regret, guilt, and doubt. The faint glimmer of sadness on E's face felt like an unspoken question, one that M couldn't bear to answer: *Had he just made the biggest mistake of his life?*

But it was too late now. The door swung shut behind them, cutting off the warmth and light of the bar, and with it, the last chance at something different. Something better. They walked into the night, the silence between them louder than any words could have been.

THE MEETING OF DEATH

The next morning, the air felt oppressive, heavy with the unspoken weight of the night before. The usual banter between M and E was absent, their enthusiasm diminished. Both men felt the gravity of the choices they had made and the path they were about to walk. But there was no time for reflection; it was time to soldier on.

Today was the day they would approach the shadow organization with their bargaining chip—the location of the Ghost. The meeting was scheduled for that afternoon in the northern outskirts of Johannesburg, at a small, dilapidated bar that exuded an air of danger.

The morning was consumed by the long drive, each mile filled with tense silence. When they finally arrived, the scene was as foreboding as they'd anticipated. Armed security personnel blended inconspicuously with the local crowd, but their watchful eyes and subtle gestures revealed their purpose. The building itself was worn and unassuming, but the tension in the air betrayed its significance.

As M and E walked through the doors, every head in the room turned to size them up. The hum of quiet conversations died instantly, leaving an eerie stillness in its wake. At the back of the bar, a man of unnerving proportions sat at a round table, radiating an aura of menace.

His name was H, a notorious crime boss whose legend preceded him. At seven feet tall, with forearms the size of tree trunks and scars crisscrossing his body, H was a living monument to violence and survival. Stories of his resilience—surviving nine close-range AK-47 shots and countless knife fights—had turned him into a near-mythical figure in South Africa's underworld.

Seated beside him was his assistant, a wiry man with sharp eyes, typing on a tablet. As M and E approached, the tension in the room became palpable. H gestured for M to sit, his massive hand pointing to a chair across the table. Without a word, he motioned for E to step aside, directing him to another table with a dismissive wave.

M met H's cold, calculating gaze and began to lay out his proposal. He spoke confidently, outlining a plan to orchestrate a multimillion-dollar life insurance fraud, promising to split the payout with H's organization while keeping a portion for himself.

H listened in silence, his scarred face revealing nothing. But when M leaned in, his voice steady, and revealed his true leverage, the atmosphere shifted.

"I have something more valuable than $30,000," M said. "I have the location of the Ghost, the codes to his vault rooms, the layout of his house, and the local police response times."

H's eyes, which had been cold and disinterested, flickered with greed. Skepticism lingered on his face, but as M presented the details, the doubt gave way to an evil smirk.

"I think we have ourselves a deal," H said, extending his hand across the table.

M took it, but before he could pull away, H's grip tightened with bone-crushing force. The sound of cracking knuckles was audible, and H's piercing gaze bore into M's soul.

"If you fuck me over," H growled, his voice low and menacing, "I'll chop you into tiny pieces and throw you down a well outside the city."

M didn't flinch, meeting H's gaze with unyielding resolve. "I wouldn't expect anything less," he replied calmly.

H finally released his grip and motioned for E to join them at the table. As E sat, H reached behind his back and pulled out a gun, placing it on the table with the barrel pointed directly at E.

"I don't like you," H said flatly, his voice dripping with suspicion. "I think you're fucking CIA."

E's face turned pale, his usual composure faltering for the first time. Before he could respond, M stepped in, his voice firm and unwavering.

"He's good, bro," M said, cutting through the tension. "He's with me."

M's heart raced as he spoke, fully aware of the truth—E *had* been approached by the CIA. But M's loyalty was unshakable, and he wouldn't allow H's paranoia to derail their plans.

"If you touch him," M added, his tone sharp and final, "the deal's off. No one harms E, or this doesn't happen. Do you understand?"

The room fell into a tense silence. H glared at M, his massive frame radiating barely contained rage. The seconds dragged on, the air thick with anticipation, until H finally leaned back and broke into a slow, menacing smile.

"We have ourselves a deal," H said at last, his voice carrying a faint hint of grudging respect.

E and M stood, the weight of the encounter pressing heavily on their shoulders. As they walked out of the bar, the oppressive tension followed them like a shadow. Neither spoke until they reached their car, the adrenaline still coursing through their veins.

They drove back to the backpackers in silence, both of them acutely aware that they had just crossed a line from which there was no return.

THE PLAN OF DYING

The plan was audacious, complex, and required an excruciating level of detail to succeed. It began with a two-week waiting period while the organization moved its pieces into place. Every aspect had to be flawless. This wasn't just a matter of orchestrating a fraud—it was about deceiving some of the most meticulous investigators in the world.

The first step involved finding a body double, a task that required an unsettling level of precision. The double had to match M's height, build, and distinguishing features, including his tattoos. Hours were spent cataloging every mark, every scar, and every detail of his skin to replicate on the stand-in. They also needed to find someone with the same blood type—a chilling necessity to pass any postmortem blood tests.

Next came a visit to a dentist, a procedure M endured with a cold, stoic detachment. His dental records were meticulously copied, with the double's teeth filed and altered to match perfectly. There was no room for error; even the slightest inconsistency could unravel the entire operation.

Then there was the matter of the vehicle. It needed to be the exact make and model of M's car, purchased under a fake name and subtly altered to pass as his own. The crash itself had to be staged with surgical precision. The car would be set ablaze, ensuring that the body was burned beyond recognition, leaving only the forensic breadcrumbs that would lead investigators to conclude that the charred remains were M.

But the scheme didn't end with the crash. Lloyd's of London, renowned for their rigorous investigative protocols, would dispatch a team to scrutinize every aspect of the incident. Their investigation could drag on for months, requiring the organization to keep M out of sight and under their control.

During this waiting period, M would be transported to a remote farm on the outskirts of Johannesburg, where he would be placed under constant armed surveillance. He would be a ghost, hidden from the world, waiting for the payout to be processed. Once the money came through, half of it would go to the organization, as agreed, and the rest—so the organization believed—would be M's to start his new life.

He would be provided with a new identity, complete with a social security number, passport, and all the paperwork required to vanish and reinvent himself. But the truth was far more complicated.

Unbeknownst to the organization, M had no intention of keeping the money for himself. Every penny of the payout was destined for his daughters. He had made peace with that decision, knowing they deserved a future, even if it meant sacrificing his own.

But that decision came with a price. M knew the moment the funds were released, his usefulness would end. The organization wouldn't let him walk away empty-handed—and he had no intention of trying. The only way out was to escape, with no money, no papers, and no plan other than to disappear into Africa and pray he could stay one step ahead of the organization's reach.

The thought of what would happen if he failed—the inevitable and horrifying consequences—hovered in the back of his mind like a dark cloud. But M shoved it aside, forcing himself to focus on the present. Fear was a luxury he couldn't afford. It clouded judgment, invited hesitation, and M knew hesitation could cost him his life.

For now, he compartmentalized. The plan was in motion, and there was no turning back. Every detail, every moment of those two weeks, had to be about survival and strategy. He would deal with the farm, the escape, and the aftermath when the time came. Until then, M kept his fears locked away, determined to see this through—if not for himself, then for the people he loved.

TWO BECAME FOUR

From this point forward, M had nothing left to lose. The knowledge of his impending death weighed heavily on him, gnawing at the edges of his mind, but instead of retreating, he allowed it to fuel a descent into a darkness he never imagined himself capable of. Every move felt like walking a razor's edge, and he embraced the recklessness that came with having nothing left to protect—except, perhaps, the faint hope of finishing what he'd started.

E, ever the opportunist, continued to work every angle to break into the diamond trade, navigating the labyrinthine criminal underworld with a mix of charm and sheer determination. He played every road, legal and illegal, in pursuit of his goal, knowing that in their world, success rarely came clean. M, for his part, threw himself into the effort, assisting E in any way he could, seeing it as a distraction from the void that had taken hold of his heart.

One day, their paths crossed with a man named J. A South African kickboxer with a fighter's physique and a demeanor as cold and unyielding as the Antarctic tundra, J carried an air of menace that was impossible to ignore. His pale, predatory eyes seemed to cut through people, as if he were constantly assessing threats and weaknesses. He promised E the contacts he needed to push further into the diamond trade, but his offers came with an unspoken edge—a sense that his help would come at a cost.

As the days bled into nights, M and E's circle grew to include others, each as enigmatic and hardened by life as the last. There was Johan, a rugged local from Johannesburg who seemed carved from stone. Weathered and formidable, Johan was a man who carried his past like a badge, every scar and story etched into his being. His constant companion was Oulu, a massive white pit bull with a presence as imposing as his owner's. Together, they were a force to be reckoned with, moving through the streets of Jo'burg with a primal intensity that demanded respect.

Then there was Susie, a Chinese-American whose path to Johannesburg seemed as improbable as it was intriguing. She had made her fortune in the cutthroat Las Vegas real estate market, accumulating wealth and power with a shrewdness that belied her adventurous spirit. Now, she traveled Africa in search of something more elusive—adventure, danger, and the kind of men who lived on the edge of reason. She exuded confidence and charisma, her sharp wit and fearless demeanor making her an unlikely yet magnetic addition to the group.

Together, this ragtag collective navigated the murky waters of Johannesburg's criminal underbelly, each bringing their unique skills and perspectives to the table. For M, their companionship was both a distraction and a reminder of how far he'd fallen. He wasn't sure whether he saw them as allies, obstacles, or merely reflections of his own fractured state.

But beneath the surface, something began to stir. Amid the chaos, the violence, and the relentless push toward survival, M started to see glimmers of something else—of redemption, of the possibility that even in darkness, there might still be a path to light.

For now, though, survival came first; and every step forward felt like another wager with fate, one he was willing to take, even if it cost him everything.

THE LONGEST DAY

It was one of those blistering, unforgiving days in northern Johannesburg—the kind where the sun clung to the sky with an almost cruel persistence, baking the earth and the people beneath it. E, M, Johan, J, and the massive dog, Oulu, squeezed into a compact rental car, its engine already straining under the weight of its passengers. They were headed out on what seemed to be a lighthearted adventure: a hunt for the mythical Val Dam, a place whose elusiveness had already turned it into a running joke between E and M. Spirits were high as they set out, the African countryside sprawling endlessly before them. Little did they know, the next forty-eight hours would unravel into some of the most brutal, heart-wrenching, and violent experiences of their lives—events that would leave scars etched not only on their bodies but also on their souls.

All four men were no strangers to chaos. They were battle-hardened, each carrying their own burdens from years of exposure to violence and suffering. But nothing in their pasts could have prepared them for the horrors they were about to witness—horrors that would reveal just how dark humanity can become when consumed by hate. This journey was to be a lesson, albeit a devastating one: a stark reminder of what happens when love and empathy are replaced by fear and malice.

The morning began innocently enough, with the group aimlessly navigating the countryside, stopping for directions that seemed only to add to the confusion. Unbeknownst to M and E, J had an ulterior motive. Under the guise of the road trip, he was quietly seeking out a connection to procure crack cocaine and brown-brown—a potent and dangerous mixture of cocaine and gunpowder. By noon, frustration had begun to set in, and the men, tired of driving, stopped at a house in a suburban area of Johannesburg.

The house belonged to one of J's contacts, an ex-mobster and former lieutenant in one of South Africa's most violent crime syndicates. A battle-scarred man with a commanding presence, he greeted them warmly, introducing his wife and young son, who was playing in an in-ground pool in the backyard. The juxtaposition was jarring: a family scene so serene and ordinary, set against the backdrop of a man whose past was steeped in blood and violence. As the wife prepared braai in the backyard, the men sipped beers around a picnic table, discussing plans.

J, in hushed tones, began filling the ex-mobster in on the life insurance schemes M and E were involved in as well as the shadowy organization that was facilitating their endeavors. The man's demeanor shifted. His expression darkened as he cautioned them, his voice grave. "You don't cross them," he warned. "If you're not serious, if you make even one mistake, you'll be dead before you know it. And it won't be quick."

After lunch, they thanked their host and piled back into the car, still no closer to finding the elusive Val Dam. Johan suggested they head back to his small cinder-block house in a rough area of Johannesburg. By midafternoon, they arrived, relieved to stretch their legs.

Later that evening, Johan proposed a visit to a members-only bar known to be a gathering place for the South African Recces, an elite group of battle-hardened soldiers renowned for their bravery and loyalty. As the men changed into fresh clothes, M realized he had forgotten his backpack. Johan walked over to a wooden box in the corner, pulling out a tattered brown-green military sweatshirt and dark canvas pants. "These belonged to my best friend," Johan said, his voice heavy with emotion. "He died fighting."

M hesitated. He didn't want to dishonor the memory of a fallen soldier by wearing the uniform. But Johan insisted, saying it would be an honor for him to wear it in his friend's memory. Reluctantly, M agreed, slipping on the uniform. It fit perfectly, though the weight of its history felt heavy on his shoulders.

The bar was exactly as described—a smoky, dimly lit room filled with men who carried themselves with the unmistakable air of seasoned warriors. As M walked in wearing the uniform, the room fell silent. Several men stood, their eyes narrowing as they approached. One of them, his voice like gravel, growled, "Who the fuck do you think you are, wearing that? Are you trying to get yourself killed?"

M met their stares with unwavering respect. He explained the gesture Johan had made and assured them he understood the gravity of what the uniform represented. Gradually, the tension eased. E and M shared their own military experiences, and soon, the room was alive with camaraderie as they swapped war stories over rounds of drinks. When it was time to leave, handshakes and hugs were exchanged, and the men were welcomed as brothers.

As they left the bar, they stopped at a petrol station to fuel up. Outside, a tall, muscular man stood leaning against a wall, his face and body covered in scars. He wore a faded USMC shirt, and his presence was impossible to ignore. Intrigued, E and M approached him. Introducing himself only as "the Marine," he revealed that he was a former sniper who had served in Sarajevo and other brutal conflicts. Now working with the Peace Corps, he was looking to reconnect with the adrenaline of his past. When he asked if he could join their group, they agreed.

Now five men and a massive dog squeezed into the tiny car, with one of them crammed into the trunk. It was nearing midnight when they found themselves in a part of Johannesburg notorious for its danger: the MTM taxi rank, a sprawling intersection teeming with minibuses, taxis, and people packed shoulder to shoulder. The air was thick with tension, and the realization of their mistake settled heavily over them. They were deep in a no-go zone for white men, especially at this hour.

Suddenly, a minibus slammed on its brakes and reversed into their car, trapping them. The crowd turned toward them, shouts rising as masked men armed with makeshift weapons closed in. Panic gripped the car. Johan whispered, "We're all going to fucking die." E's knuckles turned white on the steering wheel, his eyes fixed ahead. The Marine, calm but focused, pulled a large fixed-blade knife from his pocket as he said, "I ain't goin out like this."

"Drive!" M shouted. "Fucking drive!"

E floored the accelerator, smashing into the crowd. The car lurched forward, sending bodies sprawling. A man jumped onto the hood, stomping on the windshield as others pounded on the windows. Without hesitation, M leaned out the window, grabbed the man by the hair, and drove the knife into his neck repeatedly, blood spraying across the glass. Gunshots rang out, Molotov cocktails ignited flames, and the chaos reached a fever pitch as they tore through the crowd.

Bullets slammed into the car, one narrowly missing E. Finally, after what felt like an eternity, they broke free, speeding out of the area as the city's chaos faded into the distance. Forty-five minutes later, they pulled into Johan's driveway, the car smoking and riddled with bullet holes. The men sat in stunned silence, the gravity of what had just happened sinking in.

This night would haunt them forever—a visceral reminder of humanity's capacity for both unimaginable cruelty and relentless survival. It was a night that underscored the importance of love, empathy, and the choices we make when faced with hate.

The night seemed deceptively calm as the men stood in the front yard of Johan's small home. The air was thick with the smell of the city, and the silence carried an uneasy weight. They had no idea that the hours ahead would plunge them into an abyss of violence and terror that none of them could have imagined, even with their hardened pasts. This night would test their limits and reveal the extremes of human cruelty—and, in the midst of it, the fragile flicker of humanity that sometimes shines brightest in the darkest of moments.

For about thirty minutes, they lingered, decompressing from the earlier chaos and debating their next move. J, restless as ever, leaned back in his chair, an unlit cigarette dangling from his lips. "I know somewhere we can go. A place that'll be fun—and maybe you could make some useful contacts, M."

E and Johan both shook their heads emphatically. "Bad idea," E said firmly. "It's late, and we've already had enough for one day."

M, however, was running on empty. He felt he had nothing left to lose. With a resigned shrug, he turned to J. "Fuck it. Let's go."

The decision was made. M and J climbed into a taxi, leaving the others behind. Their destination was a place J called *The Eagle Claw*—a notorious brothel infamous not only for its debauchery but also for being a hub of South Africa's darkest trades: arms dealing, human trafficking, drugs, and other unthinkable evils. As the taxi rolled through the night,

M felt a pit forming in his stomach. Something about this felt wrong, but he pushed the thought aside.

When they arrived, the scene was as intimidating as it was surreal. Giant iron gates creaked open, revealing a courtyard surrounded by high stone walls. Armed guards flanked the entrance, their AK-47s gleaming under the dim lights. They wore body armor, and their faces were expressionless, like statues of violence. The gates slammed shut behind them with a resounding finality, and M felt a chill run down his spine.

Inside, the brothel was a hive of activity. The music was loud, the lights dim, and the air heavy with the scent of sweat, alcohol, and despair. A man greeted J at the door, his face twisted in a mix of surprise and amusement. "J? What the fuck are you doing here? Thought you were dead."

"Not yet," J replied with a laugh. Then turning to M, he said, "Wait for me at the bar. I've got business upstairs."

And with that, J disappeared, leaving M to navigate the chaos alone. Feeling exposed, M made his way to the bar and ordered a beer. He was immediately approached by several women, their intentions clear. Their curiosity was piqued by his presence—he didn't look like he belonged there, and his guarded demeanor set him apart. They bombarded him with questions, but M kept his answers short and polite. He declined every proposition, knowing the risks of disease and worse.

One of the women offered him a line of cocaine. Hesitating briefly, M decided to indulge. The numbing rush hit him almost instantly, and he decided to step outside for fresh air to clear his head. He walked into the courtyard, where the guards were stationed, their weapons casually slung across their chests. Striking up a conversation with one of them, M tried to distract himself from the gnawing unease that had settled in his gut.

As they chatted, M noticed a couple walking down the deserted street outside the gates, hand in hand. They looked peaceful, lost in their own world. But then one of the guards leaned over to M and whispered, "Watch this—they're going to die."

Startled, M turned to him. "What the hell are you talking about?"

The guard pointed down the street. "There's a gang in the bushes ahead. They've been waiting."

Instinctively, M moved toward the gate, his heart pounding with the urge to warn the couple. But before he could act, the cold barrel of an AK-47 pressed against his temple. "You open that gate, and I'll blow your brains out right here," the guard said, his voice chillingly calm. Another guard stepped behind him, ensuring there was no escape. "You're going to watch, *punk*. That's all you can do."

M froze, his teeth grinding as the seconds stretched into eternity. The couple continued walking, oblivious to the danger. Suddenly, seven men exploded from the bushes, machetes glinting in the dim streetlights. The first blow came swiftly, striking the man's arm and severing his hand. He screamed in agony, reaching out to shield himself, but the next strike came down on his face, silencing him forever.

The woman's screams pierced the night, a sound so raw and primal it seemed to shake the air itself. What followed was unspeakable—a horror that defied comprehension. The gang descended on her with merciless violence, their laughter echoing as they tore her apart piece by piece. M stood there, paralyzed, fighting the bile rising in his throat. Tears welled in his eyes, but he refused to let them fall. He couldn't look away, no matter how desperately he wanted to.

When it was over, the couple's mutilated bodies lay discarded in the street, their blood pooling beneath them like dark shadows. The gang melted back into the night, their cruel laughter fading into the distance. The silence that followed was deafening.

M's rage boiled over. He turned to the guard who still held the gun to his head. Grabbing the barrel, he pressed it against his forehead, his eyes blazing. "Fuck you. You're a fucking coward. How could you let that happen? How could you stand there and do nothing? If you're going to kill me, do it now."

The guard's expression remained unreadable as he chambered a round, the safety clicking off. His finger hovered over the trigger, but before he could pull it, J burst out of the building. "What the hell is going on out here?" he shouted, his voice cutting through the tension. "He's with me. Don't fucking touch him."

The guard hesitated then lowered his weapon, muttering something under his breath. J stormed over, shoving the guard aside. "Open the gate. We're leaving."

The gates creaked open, and M followed J out, his legs trembling with adrenaline. As they walked away, a man from inside the compound yelled, "Stop them! Don't let them leave!" The guards hesitated, but J and M were already running.

"What the fuck did you do?" M demanded as they sprinted down the street.

J grinned wickedly. "Nothing major. Just stole a sack of drugs and killed a hooker. Don't worry about it."

Behind them, engines roared to life, and headlights lit up the street. Cars screeched out of the compound, the chase underway. J leapt over the bloodied corpses in the road without a second glance, but M couldn't help but look down as he ran, the sight searing itself into his memory.

As they disappeared into the night, the weight of what he had witnessed bore down on M. The cruelty he had seen was a stark reminder of the darkness humanity is capable of—but even in the midst of that darkness, the flame of defiance and humanity still flickered.

This night would change him forever.

J and M sprinted through the labyrinthine streets of the city, their breaths ragged, their legs screaming with pain. The night wrapped around them like a suffocating shroud, every shadow seeming to pulse with danger. The sound of their feet pounding the pavement was drowned out by the distant roar of engines, the unmistakable sound of vehicles in pursuit. Somewhere behind them, men armed to the teeth hunted them like prey, their shouts echoing off the narrow, walled-off streets.

Every turn, every alley was a gamble—a desperate attempt to put distance between themselves and their pursuers. The city felt like it was folding in on itself, and the streets seemed endless. After over an hour of relentless running, their bodies betrayed them. Vomit streaked their clothes from exertion, and their feet were raw and bleeding, each step a spike of agony.

Finally, they collapsed together on the sidewalk, leaning against a metal gate. Their chests heaved as they gasped for air, their ears straining for any sound that might mean their end. The engines growled somewhere nearby, and shouts carried faintly in the night air. M turned to J, his face pale and streaked with sweat.

"It was nice knowing you, man," he said between breaths, his voice trembling with exhaustion. "It's been one hell of a run, but I guess this is it. Our time to die."

J wiped the bile from his chin and gave a weak laugh. "Never thought I'd go out like this," he muttered. "But I guess it had to come sometime."

The air grew still, the kind of stillness that made every sound seem amplified. Suddenly, from the shadows, a figure emerged. He was tall, his silhouette sharp against the faint glow of a distant streetlight. The man, as black as the night around him, stepped forward, shouldering an AK-47. His eyes glinted with an unreadable intensity.

"You guys need a place to hide out?" he asked, his voice low and calm, as if the chaos outside didn't concern him in the slightest.

Startled, J and M turned to look at him, their instincts screaming to be wary. They recognized his accent and knew he was Nigerian—a nationality that, in this part of the city, came with a reputation for brutality and deep ties to the criminal underworld. But what choice did they have? The men hunting them were getting closer, and staying on the street was a death sentence.

"Yeah," they said in unison, their voices heavy with desperation.

The man nodded, opened the gate, and motioned for them to follow. The heavy iron door clanged shut behind them, and he locked it with deliberate care. The sound of the bolt sliding home felt like the final punctuation on their escape—or perhaps their doom.

The man led them through a side entrance into the house. The air inside was thick with the acrid scent of cigar smoke, hanging like a fog that clung to the walls and ceilings. The room was dimly lit, the glow of a single overhead bulb casting long shadows. It felt like a scene straight out of a movie—a dark, foreboding tableau that seemed frozen in time.

At a wooden table on the far side of the room sat another man, wearing dark aviators despite the dead of night. One hand rested on a pistol; the other gripped a machete laid across the table. Between the weapons was an assortment of drugs: crack cocaine, heroin, pills, and powders arranged like an illicit buffet. Two other men lounged nearby, their eyes sharp, their movements slow and deliberate, like predators waiting for the right moment to strike. Milk crates lined the room's walls, their contents hidden beneath layers of grime and neglect.

M's stomach sank as he realized he had no money—his wallet was long gone, casualties of the chaos earlier in the night. But he knew the rules of a place like this: you were safe as long as you paid and used their product. Desperate, he pulled out the only thing he had left: his passport. Placing it on the table, he slid it toward the man with the aviators.

The man picked it up, flipping through its pages and glancing at the stamps from far-off places. After a moment, he sighed and tossed it back. "I have no use for this," he said flatly.

He gestured toward a side room, its windows covered in plastic sheeting, with three milk crates arranged in a rough circle in the center. "Stay there," he said, his voice devoid of emotion.

With no other options, J and M complied. They sat down, the hard edges of the crates digging into their exhausted bodies. Minutes stretched into hours, each second an eternity. They tried messaging E, but no response came. Every creak, every distant sound made their hearts race, expecting at any moment for the door to burst open and armed men to drag them out or gun them down.

The two made a pact in hushed whispers: no matter what happened, they would fight to the bitter end. If the door came crashing in, they'd take as many of their attackers as they could before they fell.

As the first rays of dawn broke over the city, the room filled with a faint, ghostly light. The sound of creaking floorboards sent a chill down their spines, and the door slowly opened. The man from the gate stood there, his AK-47 still slung over his shoulder. He looked at them for what felt like an eternity, his expression unreadable.

J and M stood, their fists clenched, ready for whatever was to come. The man's voice broke the silence. "Your ride is outside. It's by the gate. Walk straight out, get in the car, and it'll take you out of this hot zone."

M and J stared at him, stunned. No demand for money, no threats, no cruelty—just unexpected kindness in a place where they had expected none. They hesitated, unsure if it was a trick, but the man simply stepped aside, giving them space to leave.

As they walked out into the street, the warm morning sun bathed their faces, a stark contrast to the cold terror of the night before. For the first time in what felt like forever, M felt something he hadn't allowed himself to feel in years: gratitude. Whoever these men were—criminals, drug dealers, or something else entirely—they had shown him an act of humanity that defied reason.

The car waited, engine idling, and as they climbed in, M looked back at the man by the gate. Their eyes met briefly, an unspoken acknowledgment passing between them. Whatever else the day might bring, they had survived the longest night—and for that, they were grateful.

THE BIG IDEA

That evening, as the golden light of the setting sun filtered through the dusty hostel windows, M and E sat on a lopsided couch in the common room. The faint hum of a broken ceiling fan competed with the chatter of other travelers swapping stories over cheap beers. Outside, the city buzzed with life; but inside, a mischievous quiet had settled between the two friends.

The past few days had been a mix of adrenaline and chaos—an impromptu road trip, a near fistfight with an overzealous customs officer, and a business deal that had fallen through at the last moment. Now, they were left with nothing but time, dwindling cash, and their insatiable appetite for risk.

"So, what's next?" M asked, stretching out and staring at the stained ceiling. "We can't just sit here wasting time."

E leaned back, a mischievous grin spreading across his face as he swirled the last of his drink. "What if we didn't waste time? What if we went big? I'm talking big money. One job. One score."

M raised an eyebrow, intrigued but skeptical. "Go on."

E leaned forward, lowering his voice like he was about to share a secret. "We rent a plane, fly to Botswana, buy a conex full of cigarettes dirt cheap, and bootleg them back to South Africa. Cigarette smuggling is huge right now—taxes are through the roof, and the black market's booming. We could flip it for a payday of 450,000 rand."

M blinked, then laughed. "Rent a plane? Do we look like pilots to you?"

E shrugged, his grin unwavering. "Details, man. It's all in the details. We'll figure it out."

"Figure it out?" M repeated, shaking his head. "Do you even know how to fly a plane?"

"Not yet," E admitted, pulling out his phone. "But YouTube does."

M groaned, but curiosity got the better of him. He leaned over as E began searching for tutorials. Within minutes, they were watching a video titled *How to Fly a Small Aircraft: Beginner's Guide.*

"You've got to be kidding me," M muttered, but his eyes stayed glued to the screen.

The night wore on as the two of them delved deeper into their harebrained scheme. Between bursts of laughter and moments of genuine focus, they began piecing together a plan. The tutorials made flying seem deceptively simple—push this lever, pull that yoke, keep an eye on the gauges. E even took notes, sketching out the basic controls on a napkin.

By the time midnight rolled around, the idea had gone from absurd to almost plausible.

"Okay," M said, leaning back with a sigh. "Let's say, for argument's sake, we could figure out how to fly. What about the paperwork? Planes aren't exactly 'rent and go.'"

E grinned, the kind of grin that usually preceded one of his riskier ideas. "We need licenses, right? I know a guy who knows a guy."

The next morning, bleary-eyed but fueled by determination, they drove across the city to the local DMV. From the outside, it looked like any other government building—gray, unremarkable, and surrounded by a line of people waiting to renew their licenses.

"Front door or back?" E asked as they parked.

M squinted, noticing a smaller, shadier-looking line forming around the back of the building. "What's the back line for?"

"Only one way to find out."

They joined the back line, which led to a makeshift setup behind the DMV. There, a man sat at a folding table, a well-worn Xerox machine humming beside him. His sunglasses reflected the morning sun, and he looked up lazily as they approached.

"You boys looking for licenses?" he asked, not bothering to hide his disinterest.

"Depends," E replied, feigning nonchalance. "What have you got?"

The man reached into a folder and pulled out a laminated price list. "Driver's licenses, motorcycle permits, hunting licenses. You name it. Oh, and pilot's licenses."

M and E exchanged a glance. "Pilot's licenses, huh?" M said, trying to keep his voice steady.

"How much?" E asked.

The man leaned back, chewing on a toothpick. "Five hundred rand each. Extra for a rush job."

E handed over the money without hesitation. As the man fired up the Xerox machine, M leaned over and whispered, "This is insane."

"Relax," E whispered back. "Insane is where the money is."

Minutes later, they walked away with brand-new pilot's licenses that looked convincing enough to pass a casual inspection. E held his up to the sunlight, admiring it like a trophy.

"While we're here," he said, turning back to the man, "we'll take CDL licenses too. You know, just in case."

By the time they left, their wallets were lighter, but their confidence was soaring. They had the licenses, they had a plan, and they had just enough recklessness to believe they could pull it off.

"Now what?" M asked as they climbed back into the car.

"Now," E said, grinning ear to ear, "we find a plane."

The afternoon sun hung high in the sky as M and E navigated the winding roads on the outskirts of the city. The heat shimmered off the asphalt, and the smell of dry grass and distant petrol fumes filled the air. Armed with nothing more than their newly minted pilot's licenses and an unrealistic amount of optimism, they set out to find a plane they could "borrow" for their venture.

"Okay," M said, scrolling through his phone. "So far, I've found two small airports within driving distance. Both are used for crop dusters, private planes, that kind of thing."

"Perfect," E said, gripping the steering wheel with purpose. "This is going to be a piece of cake."

"Piece of cake?" M shot him a look. "We're not renting a car. This is a plane. A *plane*, E."

E waved off his concern with a casual flick of his wrist. "Details, my friend. Details. We'll just walk in, flash the licenses, and act like we've done this a million times."

The first airport they visited was a small, dusty strip on the edge of a sleepy farming town. A handful of single-engine planes were parked haphazardly near a rusting hangar, their faded paint jobs suggesting they hadn't seen much action in years.

Inside the office, a middle-aged woman sat behind a desk cluttered with papers and a mug that read *World's Okayest Pilot*. She didn't even look up as they entered.

"Hi there," E said, leaning on the counter with his best attempt at charm. "We're looking to rent a plane. Something big enough to carry a decent amount of cargo."

The woman finally glanced up, raising an eyebrow. "You boys got a license?"

E and M both produced their freshly laminated pilot's licenses, holding them up proudly.

The woman squinted at the licenses, then at them, clearly skeptical. "You've flown before, right?"

"Of course," E said, his grin unwavering. "Plenty of times."

M nodded enthusiastically. "Yeah, we're, uh…between jobs right now. Just looking for something quick."

The woman sighed and leaned back in her chair. "We don't rent to amateurs, and even if we did, I don't have anything that can carry cargo. You're better off trying somewhere else."

Back outside, M shook his head. "That went well."

"Hey, it's a process," E said, already heading for the car. "Let's try the next one."

Their second stop was a slightly larger airport just outside the city limits. Unlike the first, this one had a more professional vibe, with a handful of staff milling about and planes taxiing on the runway.

"Okay, let's try not to look like complete idiots this time," M muttered as they walked into the main office.

"Relax," E said, straightening his jacket. "Confidence is key."

This time, they were greeted by a grizzled old man wearing aviator sunglasses and a leather bomber jacket that looked like it had been through a war.

"Can I help you, boys?" he asked, his voice gravelly.

"Yes, sir," E said, stepping forward. "We're looking to rent a cargo plane for a quick job. Got any recommendations?"

The man eyed them suspiciously. "Cargo plane, huh? What kind of cargo?"

"Uh, supplies," M said quickly. "Just some, uh, humanitarian aid. You know, helping out a friend in Botswana."

The man snorted. "Humanitarian aid, my ass. You've got the look of smugglers about you."

E laughed nervously. "Smugglers? Us? No, sir, we're just…entrepreneurs."

The old man stared at them for a long moment then chuckled. "Well, you've got guts, I'll give you that. Tell you what—I've got an old Douglas C-47 Skytrain out back. She's not pretty, but she'll get the job done if you treat her right."

"Perfect!" E said, clapping his hands.

"One condition," the man added, his expression turning serious. "You wreck her, you pay for her. And if you get caught doing something stupid, I never saw you."

"Deal," E said without hesitation.

The man led them out to the tarmac, where the Douglas C-47 sat in all her faded glory. The olive-green paint was chipped and peeling, and the propellers looked like they hadn't been serviced in years.

"She's a warbird," the man said, patting the plane affectionately. "Survived more missions than I can count. If you treat her right, she'll treat you right."

M stared at the plane, equal parts awe and terror in his eyes. "We're really doing this, aren't we?"

E grinned and slapped him on the back. "Damn right we are."

After a quick and questionably thorough inspection, they finalized the rental agreement, paid in cash, and received a crash course in the plane's basic controls. They stood in front of their new ride, the reality of their plan finally sinking in.

"Next stop," E said, clapping his hands together, "Botswana."

"Let's just try not to die before we get there," M replied, shaking his head as they climbed into the cockpit.

After looking around, they climbed into the back of the plane and spent the night in restless sleep. The next morning as the sun began to light up the sky, the Douglas C-47 Skytrain roared to life with a mechanical growl, its twin radial engines sputtering and coughing as they settled into a steady rhythm. The sound reverberated through the cockpit, shaking the entire fuselage as E and M adjusted their stolen pilot's licenses on their jackets with exaggerated pride.

"Ready for this?" E asked, gripping the yoke with far more confidence than he felt.

"Absolutely not," M replied, laughing nervously. "But it's not like we're turning back now."

They taxied to the end of the runway, the small airport quiet except for the low hum of distant crickets in the early morning air. The scent of aviation fuel and the metallic tang of oil filled the cockpit as M glanced over the controls one last time, pretending he knew what half of them did.

"Throttle forward, let's go!" E shouted, a manic grin on his face.

The plane lurched forward, gaining speed painfully slowly, its heavy frame groaning under the strain. Dust and pebbles kicked up behind them as they rattled down the narrow strip, the nose pitching up unevenly. For a terrifying moment, it seemed like they'd run out of runway before liftoff, but then, with a final jolt, the Skytrain lifted into the air, breaking free from the earth's grip.

As the city below shrank away, an almost surreal calm enveloped them. The world seemed to stretch infinitely, the patchwork of brown and green fields rolling out beneath them under a vast blue sky. The distant horizon blurred into the soft orange glow of the rising sun, painting the landscape in warm hues.

"You see that?" E said, pointing out the window. "That's freedom right there."

"Yeah," M muttered, still gripping the armrest tightly. "Freedom to crash into the middle of nowhere if we screw this up."

Despite his nerves, M couldn't help but marvel at the landscape. Rivers snaked lazily across the plains, their silvery surfaces catching the sunlight. Small villages dotted the terrain, clusters of thatched-roof houses surrounded by grazing livestock. It was a view neither of them had ever seen before—a perspective that made their insane venture feel, for the first time, like a real adventure.

As they gained altitude, the plane steadied, and their earlier nerves gave way to excitement. E fiddled with the ancient GPS system, inputting the coordinates for their rendezvous in Botswana.

"Looks like we're on track," he said, leaning back in his seat and flashing M a grin. "This isn't so hard."

"Famous last words," M shot back, but even he couldn't suppress a smile.

The hours ticked by as they flew over the open countryside. They took turns at the controls, experimenting with the dials and switches like kids with a new toy. Every so often, E would tap the altimeter or adjust the throttle, pretending he knew what he was doing.

"Hey, what's this button do?" M asked, pointing to a lever near the dashboard.

"Don't touch it!" E yelled.

"Why not?"

"I don't know, but don't touch it!"

Their laughter filled the cockpit, a mixture of giddy exhilaration and disbelief that they'd come this far. They passed the time swapping stories, speculating about the money they'd make, and debating the best way to spend their fortune.

"I'm thinking a beach house," E said, gazing out at the clouds. "Someplace quiet, maybe Mozambique. What about you?"

"Honestly? A new car. Something fast," M replied. "Oh, and maybe not dying today."

As they crossed the border into Botswana, the terrain began to change. The flat plains gave way to more rugged landscapes, dotted with acacia trees and rocky outcrops. The sun climbed higher, its golden rays now bathing the land in a harsh, unforgiving light.

The GPS beeped, signaling their approach to the coordinates. E leaned forward, squinting at the screen. "We're close. Should be a landing strip around here somewhere."

"Landing strip?" M repeated, scanning the ground below. "You mean that patch of dirt that looks like it hasn't seen a plane in fifty years?"

"That's the one," E confirmed, adjusting their descent.

M tightened his seatbelt, his heart pounding as the plane began its approach. The strip was little more than a dusty clearing flanked by tall grass and a few scattered trees. As they descended, the ground rushed up to meet them faster than M expected.

"Steady…steady…," E muttered, his hands gripping the yoke tightly.

The wheels hit the ground with a jarring thud, the plane bouncing once, then twice, before finally settling into a rough roll. Dust billowed around them, obscuring their view as they skidded to a halt at the end of the makeshift runway.

M let out a shaky laugh, his knuckles white from gripping the armrest. "Well, we didn't die. I'll call that a win."

Outside, the driver of the semi waved at them, his weathered face indifferent to their dramatic arrival. The trailer behind him was loaded with box after box of cigarettes, the payload they'd come all this way to retrieve.

E shut down the engines, the sudden silence almost deafening after hours of flight. He turned to M, his grin as wide as ever. "Told you we could do it."

"Yeah, well," M replied, unbuckling his harness. "Let's see if we can do it again on the way back."

They climbed down from the cockpit, the heat of the midday sun pressing down on them as they got to work.

The plane sat in the center of the dusty landing strip, its engines silent and the air around it heavy with heat and anticipation. The rusted semitruck, a lumbering relic of another era, rumbled up alongside the plane, its cargo trailer filled to the brim with neatly stacked crates of cigarettes. The driver, a grizzled man with a sun-bleached hat and a permanent scowl, hopped out of the cab and motioned toward the trailer without saying a word.

"This is it," E said, clapping his hands together. "Our golden ticket."

M squinted at the crates as they opened the trailer's rear doors, his shirt already damp with sweat from the midday sun. "A lot of golden tickets. Hope they're worth it."

The two of them worked quickly, loading the crates into the cargo hold of the Douglas C-47. Each crate was heavier than it looked, and the process soon had them drenched in sweat and panting for air. The old semi's driver leaned against the side of his truck, chewing on a toothpick and watching them with a bemused expression.

"You boys sure about this?" he finally asked, his gravelly voice carrying a note of skepticism.

"Positive," E replied, stacking another crate with a grunt. "We've got this under control."

The driver shook his head and muttered something in Setswana before climbing back into the truck and driving off, leaving a cloud of dust in his wake.

By the time they finished loading the last crate, the sun was beginning to sink toward the horizon, casting long shadows across the runway. M wiped his brow and leaned against the plane, catching his breath. "That's a lot of cigarettes."

"That's a lot of money," E corrected, grinning as he slammed the cargo hold shut. "All we have to do is get this baby off the ground and back to South Africa."

"Yeah, because that's the easy part," M muttered, eyeing the plane nervously.

They climbed into the cockpit, the weight of the cargo causing the plane to groan slightly as it settled into the dirt. E slid into the pilot's seat, his excitement undimmed by the enormity of what they were about to attempt.

"All right," he said, flipping switches and adjusting controls with the confidence of someone who had spent at least a few hours on YouTube. "Let's fire her up."

The engines sputtered to life with a deafening roar, shaking the entire plane as they settled into a steady rhythm. Outside, the last rays of sunlight bathed the dusty strip in a fiery glow, the sky shifting to hues of orange and purple.

"Here we go," E said, gripping the yoke.

The plane began to move, lumbering down the runway like an overfed bird attempting to take flight. The extra weight of the cargo made the takeoff far more challenging than their earlier flight, and for a terrifying moment, it seemed like the runway would run out before they gained enough speed.

"Pull up! Pull up!" M shouted, gripping the armrest as the plane hurtled toward the treetops at the end of the strip.

E gritted his teeth, and they both yanked back on the yoke with all their strength. The plane's nose pitched upward just in time, the wheels grazing the top branches of the trees as they climbed into the sky.

"Ha!" E shouted, pumping his fist in triumph. "Told you we could do it!"

"Let's not celebrate yet," M said, his knuckles white as he gripped the edge of his seat. "We've got a long way to go."

As they ascended, the landscape below unfolded like a painting—rolling hills, scattered villages, and endless stretches of golden savanna bathed in the warm light of the setting sun. For a brief moment, the beauty of it all made them forget the danger of what they were doing.

The cockpit was filled with a mix of exhilaration and tension as they leveled out and set their course for the South African border. M fiddled with the radio, finally settling on Andrew W.K.'s "Party Hard" while E kept one eye on the controls and the other on the horizon.

"You think this is actually going to work?" M asked after a long silence.

"Of course it's going to work," E replied, his grin returning. "We're practically professionals now."

M snorted. "Yeah, sure. Professionals with fake licenses and a crash course in not crashing."

"Details," E said, waving him off.

The first hour of the flight went smoothly. The engines hummed steadily, and the rhythmic vibrations of the plane seemed almost soothing. They passed the time swapping jokes and speculating about how they'd spend their earnings.

But as they approached the border, the mood began to shift. M noticed it first—a faint trail of smoke curling from the starboard engine.

"Uh, E," he said, his voice tight. "We've got a problem."

E glanced out the window, his grin faltering. "Shit."

The smoke thickened, and before long, the engine sputtered and died, leaving the propeller motionless.

"We're losing altitude," M said, panic creeping into his voice.

"Relax," E said, though his knuckles were white on the yoke. "We've still got one engine. We can make it."

But as the border crossing came into view, the second engine began to falter, coughing and sputtering like it, too, was ready to give up.

"This isn't happening," E muttered, frantically adjusting the controls.

"It's happening," M said, unbuckling his harness. "We're going down."

The cockpit was chaos. Warning lights flashed on the dashboard, and the remaining engine sputtered violently, threatening to quit at any moment. The plane lurched and groaned, its weight pulling it down faster than E and M could compensate.

"This is it!" E shouted over the roar of the wind tearing through the cockpit. "We're not going to make it!"

"No kidding!" M yelled back, already fumbling with the parachute pack he'd yanked from the compartment behind his seat. His hands trembled as he cinched the straps around his shoulders. "Do you even know if these things are packed, right?"

"Does it matter? It's this or go down with the plane!" E snapped, grabbing his own parachute and struggling to secure it.

The horizon tilted sharply as the plane began to bank uncontrollably. Below them, the South African border crossing came into view, a cluster of buildings and vehicles that grew larger with every passing second. M could make out tiny figures on the ground pointing up at the plummeting aircraft.

E pulled open the side door of the cockpit, and a deafening rush of wind nearly yanked him off his feet. The noise was overwhelming, a cacophony of engines dying, air screaming past the fuselage.

"Ready?" E shouted, gripping the door frame for balance.

"Fuck yes!" M yelled, but he tightened his grip on the doorframe, his heart pounding like a drum.

Without another word, E threw himself into the void, his body vanishing into the open sky.

"God help me," M muttered before following suit, the wind tearing at him as he leaped from the doomed plane.

For a moment, there was nothing but freefall—a dizzying rush of air and adrenaline as the ground hurtled toward him.

The parachute jerked him upward with a violent tug, the straps biting into his shoulders. His descent slowed, and he took a shaky breath, glancing around to find E. A few hundred yards away, E was descending as well, his parachute flapping in the wind.

Below them, the plane was a fiery comet streaking toward the earth. It tilted into a sharp bank before slamming into the ground with a deafening explosion. A fireball erupted, sending plumes of smoke and debris into the air.

"So much for our payday," M muttered to himself as he floated toward the ground.

The chaos on the ground was immediate. Vehicles from the border crossing raced toward the crash site, their sirens wailing. Soldiers and guards poured out, weapons in hand, scanning the sky for any sign of survivors.

M landed hard, his feet hitting the dry, rocky earth with enough force to knock the wind out of him. He scrambled to his feet, yanking off the parachute and scanning the horizon for E.

"Over here!" E's voice called, and M turned to see him sprinting toward the nearest patch of dense bush.

They didn't waste time talking. Both knew the border guards wouldn't take long to realize what had happened, and their best chance was to disappear into the wilderness before anyone could track them down.

The sun was sinking fast, casting long shadows across the landscape and bathing everything in hues of orange and red. The air was thick with the acrid smell of smoke from the crash, and the distant shouts of the guards spurred them onward.

"How far do you think we can get before they find us?" M asked, his voice hoarse from exertion.

"Far enough," E replied, ducking under a low-hanging branch. "If we keep moving, they'll have a hard time tracking us in the dark."

The terrain was unforgiving—thorny shrubs, uneven ground, and patches of dry grass that crunched loudly underfoot. Every sound seemed magnified, every rustle of leaves a potential threat.

As night fell, the stars emerged, casting a dim light over the bush. The distant glow of flashlights and the occasional bark of a guard dog reminded them how close danger still was.

"We need water," E whispered as they paused to catch their breath behind a large boulder.

"First, we need distance," M replied, peering over the rock. "If we can get to the river, we'll have a better chance of losing them."

They pressed on, their movements growing slower and more deliberate as exhaustion set in. The guards' voices faded into the distance replaced by the sounds of the night—crickets chirping, the rustle of leaves in the breeze, and the occasional call of a distant animal.

When they finally reached the river, the cool water was a godsend. They drank deeply, washing the dust and sweat from their faces before wading into the shallows to mask their trail.

As they sat on the far bank, catching their breath and watching the flicker of distant searchlights on the horizon, M shook his head and laughed softly.

"What's so funny?" E asked, his voice low.

"All that work," M said, gesturing toward the distant plume of smoke. "And it all went up in flames. Literally."

E chuckled, leaning back against a tree. "Yeah, well. At least you're supposed to die soon."

"Haha, that's funny," M muttered.

"But being alive is a good start," E replied, staring up at the stars. "We'll figure the rest out."

For now, they were safe—battered, exhausted, and penniless, but alive.

TIME FOR M TO DIE

The day had finally come. After two grueling weeks that felt like an eternity, M stood in the small room he had called home during this pivotal period. The air was thick with anticipation, and his thoughts swirled like a storm. These two weeks had been a whirlwind of preparation, strategy, and sleepless nights—yet now, looking back, they seemed to have passed in the blink of an eye.

As he gathered his belongings—a few essentials thrown into a worn duffel bag—the weight of reality hit him like a freight train. This wasn't some theoretical plan anymore. The moment he crossed the threshold of this room, there was no going back. Every action he'd taken, every decision he'd made had led to this day.

He paused for a moment, his hands gripping the bag tightly. *This is real*, he thought. *This is happening.* A knot formed in his stomach, but he shoved the doubt aside. There wasn't room for hesitation—not now. He'd come too far.

E was waiting for him outside, leaning casually against the car, his expression calm and collected as always. He flashed a grin when he saw M step out, but there was a flicker of tension in his eyes that betrayed his usual bravado.

"Ready for this?" E asked, his voice light but laced with an undertone of seriousness.

"Do I have a choice?" M replied, tossing his bag into the back seat.

E chuckled, shaking his head. "Not really."

The drive to the meeting site was quiet, the air between them heavy with unspoken thoughts. The faint hum of the engine and the rhythmic sound of tires on the road did little to ease the tension. Outside, the world seemed indifferent to the storm raging within M's mind. The sun was just beginning to rise, casting long shadows across the empty streets and painting the sky in hues of orange and pink.

M stared out the window, his mind racing. He thought about the endless hours spent planning, the sacrifices made, the risks taken. Every detail of the plan had been scrutinized, every contingency considered—yet the nagging voice in the back of his mind whispered that something was off.

"Hard to believe we're here, huh?" E said, breaking the silence.

"Yeah," M replied, his voice quieter than he intended. "Hard to believe."

As they neared the meeting site, the surroundings grew more desolate. The vibrant city streets gave way to industrial buildings and vacant lots, their shadows looming large in the early morning light. When they pulled into the gravel parking lot, M felt a chill run down his spine.

The warehouse stood in stark contrast to the quiet dawn. Its corrugated metal walls were streaked with rust, and a faint smell of oil and decay hung in the air. Three armed men stood outside, their postures stiff and their faces expressionless.

"Here we go," E muttered, killing the engine.

M took a deep breath as they stepped out of the car. The crunch of gravel underfoot sounded unnaturally loud in the stillness. The men outside watched them closely, their hands resting on the weapons slung across their chests.

"Follow us," one of them said gruffly, gesturing toward the building.

The two friends exchanged a quick glance before complying. Inside, the air was cooler but no less oppressive. They were led through a maze of dimly lit corridors, the sound of their footsteps echoing against the concrete walls. Each step seemed to amplify M's growing sense of unease.

Finally, they were ushered into a small, windowless room. A single table with two chairs sat in the center, its stark simplicity doing nothing to dispel the tension. The fluorescent light overhead flickered faintly, casting harsh shadows that made the space feel even smaller.

M and E barely had time to take in their surroundings before one of the armed men entered the room. He was tall and broad-shouldered, his face scarred and his expression cold. He stood in front of them, his gaze piercing as it settled on M.

"There's been a change of plans," he said, his voice low and deliberate.

M felt his stomach drop.

His cold voice slicing through the tension in the room like a blade.

M felt the air shift, heavy and foreboding. Every muscle in his body tensed, his instincts screaming at him that something was horribly wrong.

The man reached into his waistband, pulling out a chrome Colt 45. The metallic glint of the weapon caught the harsh fluorescent light, sending an involuntary chill down M's spine. Slowly, methodically, the man ejected the magazine, leaving a single round in the chamber.

He placed the gun on the table, his movements deliberate, almost ritualistic. With a nod toward E, he said, "Kill him. He's going to be your body double now."

The words hung in the air, surreal and suffocating.

M froze, his mind racing to make sense of the situation. Time seemed to warp, every second stretching into an eternity. He glanced at E, whose face was pale, his wide eyes betraying the terror he was trying to suppress.

I've only known him for a few weeks, he thought, his mind a storm of conflicting emotions. *We've been through a lot, sure, but this?* The room suddenly felt smaller, the walls pressing in on him.

E was family now. Blood didn't matter—this was his brother, his ride-or-die. M's heart steadied as clarity replaced the panic. *We either walk out of here together or not at all.*

With a deep breath, M reached for the gun. His movements were slow and deliberate, his expression giving nothing away. The man's steely eyes tracked every move, but M refused to waver.

As his hand wrapped around the cool metal, M made his decision. In one fluid motion, he raised the weapon and fired. The deafening crack of the shot echoed off the concrete walls as the round struck its target squarely in the forehead. Blood and bits of bone sprayed across the table as the man crumpled to the floor, his lifeless body hitting the ground with a sickening thud.

The room erupted into chaos.

Before the first man's body hit the floor, E lunged at the second guard, grabbing the rifle slung over his shoulder. A struggle ensued, the barrel jerking wildly as both men fought for control. E ripped the rifle free and unloaded half the magazine into the man's chest spraying blood and flesh across the floor.

M pivoted toward the third man, who was already raising his weapon. M lunged forward, grabbing the rifle and wrestling with the man as the gun discharged, sending bullets into the ceiling and walls. The acrid smell of gunpowder filled the room, mingling with the metallic tang of blood.

E, holding the first guard's rifle, acted quickly. He turned the weapon on M's assailant and fired three precise shots into the man's torso. The guard staggered backward, his grip slackening before he collapsed to the ground. For good measure or out of anger, M fired five more shots into the man's head, turning it into a mangled mess of flesh.

The room fell silent except for the ragged breaths of M and E.

"You good?" E asked, his voice hoarse.

M nodded, wiping the blood from his face with his sleeve. "Yeah. Let's get the hell out of here."

They moved quickly, grabbing extra magazines and anything else useful from the guards' gear. E checked the hallway through the cracked door before motioning for M to follow.

The two sprinted down the dimly lit corridors, the adrenaline coursing through their veins propelling them forward. The warehouse was no longer silent; distant shouts and the sound of heavy footsteps echoed through the halls.

Bursting out into the parking lot, they made a beeline for their car. E jumped into the driver's seat, slamming the door as M dove into the passenger side.

"Go!" M shouted, his voice tinged with urgency.

E floored the accelerator, the tires screeching against the gravel as the car fishtailed out of the lot.

Behind them, the warehouse exploded into activity. More armed men poured out, shouting and pointing as they raised their weapons. M ducked as bullets pinged off the car's frame, the rear window shattering in a spray of glass.

"Keep it steady!" M yelled, loading a fresh magazine into his newly acquired rifle.

E gritted his teeth, his knuckles white on the steering wheel as he swerved onto the main road.

"They're gaining on us!" M shouted, glancing over his shoulder as he fired his AK-47 back at the pursuing vehicles.

In the rearview mirror, they could see the headlights of the pursuing vehicles closing in. The distant glow of muzzle flashes lit up the night as their pursuers fired relentlessly.

"We've got to lose them!" M said, his voice strained.

"I'm working on it!" E snapped, his focus unyielding.

The chase led them through narrow streets and abandoned industrial zones, the car's tires screeching with every sharp turn. E's driving was erratic but effective, the gaps between them and their pursuers widening with each maneuver.

Finally, after what felt like an eternity, they reached the outskirts of the city. The dim glow of streetlights gave way to the open darkness of the countryside. E veered off the main road, guiding the car down a dirt path flanked by dense brush.

They killed the headlights and coasted to a stop, the engine ticking softly in the quiet night.

"Do you think we lost them?" M asked, his voice barely above a whisper.

"Let's hope so," E replied, his grip on the wheel relaxing for the first time.

They sat in silence, the weight of what had just happened settling over them. M stared out at the dark horizon, his mind replaying the events in vivid detail.

"We shouldn't be alive right now," he finally said.

E leaned back, letting out a shaky laugh. "Yeah, well, I guess we're just too stubborn to die."

M couldn't help but smile, despite everything. They had survived—together. And in that moment, nothing else mattered.

E sat in the driver's seat, staring straight ahead, his hands motionless on the steering wheel. The dim glow from the dashboard reflected off his face, hollow with disbelief. All M's money, all his time, every meticulous detail he had planned—it was all gone. Months of preparation obliterated in a matter of minutes. Now, as they sat in the silence of the car, it felt like the whole world was closing in.

Beside him, M slumped in the passenger seat, breathing heavily, his face streaked with dirt and sweat. The tension between them was thick, but neither said a word. There wasn't much to say. They both knew what was happening out there.

The word had already started to spread, slithering through the darkest corners of the underworld, carried by whispers and encrypted messages. A bounty had been placed—*350,000 rand*. Enough to make even the most reluctant predator come out of the shadows.

E finally broke the silence, his voice hoarse, like he was afraid even the car might betray them. "That bounty's no joke, M. Everyone's going to be coming for us now."

M didn't respond, his jaw tightening as he stared blankly out the windshield. He had been warned, but he hadn't believed it would come to this. His plan was supposed to be airtight, flawless. He had accounted for everything—except this.

Minutes ticked by in silence, the weight of their predicament settling on them like a storm cloud. E glanced at M, his expression unreadable; and then, in a voice barely louder than a whisper, he said, "Thanks for not letting me die, man."

M turned his head slightly, meeting E's eyes. There was a flicker of something there—guilt, maybe, or gratitude. But all he said was, "You're welcome."

As the words hung in the air, E tightened his grip on the wheel. The plan might be in ruins, but it wasn't over. Not yet. If there was one thing M knew, it was how to survive. And as long as they were still breathing, there was still a chance to fix this—or at least go down fighting.

PLAN Z AND A MURDERED BABY

E and M needed to figure out their next move. After a tense discussion, they decided to head back to Melville—a risky decision, but one that offered some familiarity and resources they desperately needed. Once back in Melville, they unexpectedly ran into their friend Susie. True to her fiery and fearless nature, she insisted on joining them despite the evident dangers. M tried to dissuade her, but Susie wasn't the type to take no for an answer.

E managed to secure a safe house—a modest but secure building located just a ten-minute drive from their usual haunt, the Home Base Hostel. The property had a high-walled courtyard, an iron gate, and was completely off the grid as far as anyone knew. For now, it was their best chance at lying low.

Their first night in the safe house was anything but restful. The house was barren, with no furniture to ease their exhaustion. The three of them sat on the cold, tiled floors, sharing uneasy glances, their nerves frayed from the events of the day. M tried to sleep near the front door, keeping his handgun within reach, while E and Susie retreated to the back room.

But sleep was elusive, not because of their stress but because of the haunting cries of a small child coming from the neighboring house just a few feet away. The crying was relentless, piercing through the quiet night like a knife. Hours crawled by, and the sound seemed to burrow into their bones, amplifying their already raw emotions. M found himself gripping his handgun tighter with each passing hour, feeling powerless against the cries that wouldn't stop.

Finally, in the early hours of the morning, the crying ceased. A heavy, almost unnatural silence settled over the neighborhood. E and Susie, who had finally drifted off in the back room, were oblivious to the shift in the air. M, still awake in the living room near the front door, tried to convince himself that it was nothing—just exhaustion and paranoia playing tricks on his mind.

But then out of nowhere, there was a knock.

The sound sent a jolt through M's entire body. He shot upright, heart pounding, grabbing the handgun that lay beside him. Every nerve in his body screamed that this was it—the worst-case scenario had arrived. Slowly, he approached the solid front door, his pulse hammering in his ears. He unlocked it cautiously, keeping the iron-barred security door firmly closed as he peered through the narrow gap.

What he saw made his stomach churn.

Standing on the other side of the security door was a large, hulking man, completely naked. His gaunt face was twisted in a grotesque expression, his body smeared with dirt and blood. But the thing that made M's stomach lurch and bile rise in his throat was what the man had impaled on his privates—something unspeakable, something M didn't want to believe was real. It was the man's infant child.

A wave of realization crashed over him, and his legs nearly buckled beneath him. The cries from the night before—the heartbreaking wails of that child—suddenly made horrifying sense.

M froze, unable to move, his mind screaming at him to do something, anything, but his body refused to cooperate. The man stood there, leering, swaying slightly as if waiting for M to act.

Then like a ghost moving through the shadows, E appeared behind M. His hand passed smoothly over M's shoulder, Glock steady in his grip.

There was no hesitation.

BLAM!

The deafening gunshot reverberated through the small house, the sound so loud it felt like it ruptured M's eardrum. The man crumpled to the ground outside, his grotesque form illuminated briefly by the porch light before the night swallowed him whole.

M stumbled back, gasping for air, his legs trembling. The gunshot had jolted him back to reality, but the horror of what he had just witnessed lingered like a dark shadow in his mind. E turned to him, his face grim but composed.

"We'll figure this out later," E said quietly, his voice steady but cold. "Right now, we survive."

M nodded, swallowing the lump in his throat as he gripped the handgun tighter. He couldn't shake the image of the man at the door or the cries of the child that would haunt his dreams for nights to come.

But E was right. Whatever came next, they needed to survive.

Susie stumbled out of the back room, barefoot and wide-eyed, drawn by the deafening gunshot that shattered the fragile stillness of the house. She skidded to a stop at the front door, gripping the frame as she peered out through the iron bars of the security door. The sight before her was more than her mind could process.

Her knees buckled, and she doubled over as a guttural wail escaped her lips, raw and primal. Tears streamed down her face, blurring her vision as she heaved violently, vomiting onto the cold floor. Between gasps for air, she managed to choke out, "How…how could someone do that? How could there be such evil in the world?" Her body trembled uncontrollably, tears wracking her frame as she clutched her chest, trying to contain the overwhelming wave of horror and grief.

M stood nearby, his face pale and taut, struggling to maintain composure. His voice was steady but firm when he spoke. "We have to call this in. Someone will have heard the shot."

E nodded grimly, pulling out his cell phone with hands that shook ever so slightly. His face was unreadable, a mask of grim determination as he dialed the number for the local police department. The phone rang once, twice, and then a voice on the other end picked up.

"There's been a shooting," E said, his voice low but firm. He provided the address, keeping his explanation as vague as possible. He hung up without waiting for questions, his focus already on what needed to be done next.

Minutes later, the faint wail of sirens reached their ears, growing louder as a squad car pulled up in front of the house. Two officers stepped out, their expressions already hardened with suspicion. They approached cautiously, their hands hovering near their holstered weapons as E and M opened the door.

The officers stepped onto the porch and froze as their eyes landed on the gruesome scene just a few feet away. The taller of the two let out a sharp exhale, muttering something under his breath as he turned his head away, briefly shielding his face. The younger officer's face twitched as he fought to maintain a stoic expression, but the color drained from his cheeks as he stood there, staring.

After a long, tense moment, the taller officer finally turned to E and M, his tone cold and matter-of-fact. "Here's how this is going to work," he said, his words cutting through the tension like a blade. "You get rid of the body. We'll look the other way."

Susie gasped audibly from behind M, her tear-streaked face twisted in disbelief. "What?" she stammered, but the officer ignored her, already turning back toward the squad car.

"Just make it disappear," the younger officer added quietly, avoiding eye contact as he followed his partner.

Without another word, the two officers climbed back into their vehicle and drove off, their red and blue lights vanishing into the darkness.

M and E exchanged a long look, the weight of the situation pressing heavily on both of them. They didn't have time to process what had just happened or the officers' chilling indifference. The priority was clear: they had to act, and fast.

Working quickly and efficiently, M and E moved to clean up the scene, their movements mechanical and precise, as if detaching themselves from the reality of what they were doing. The stench, the blood, the weight of the lifeless forms—they forced it all to the back of their minds, focusing only on finishing the task before dawn.

Susie sat huddled in the corner of the living room, her knees drawn up to her chest, sobbing softly into her arms. She didn't dare look at what they were doing; the mere sound of their footsteps and the rustle of the tarp was enough to make her stomach churn again.

When the job was done, E and M silently packed their bags, their faces set with grim resolve. They knew the safe house was compromised. The gunshot would have been enough to attract unwanted attention, but now, they had a body to dispose of and a neighborhood on edge. Staying wasn't an option.

As the first light of dawn crept over the horizon, they slipped out of the house, their belongings slung over their shoulders, and disappeared into the shadows. They didn't speak as they walked away, their minds too preoccupied with what lay ahead. They had no plan, no destination—only the understanding that the clock was ticking and survival depended on staying one step ahead of the chaos they had left behind.

ESCAPE TO THE CAPE

Susie, E, and M decided their best chance at escaping the growing danger was to make their way to Johannesburg's airport and catch a flight to Cape Town. The plan was simple: avoid detection, get on the plane, and regroup once they were safely on the other side of the country. But as they approached the airport, M's stomach churned.

From a distance, he spotted them—several men from the organization, blending into the bustling crowd at the entrance. They weren't just loitering; they were watching, scanning every face that passed, their sharp eyes hunting for one in particular: M.

He was the one with the bounty: *350,000 rand*. A sum big enough to turn even strangers into enemies. The very thought made his palms sweat. E and Susie were at risk simply by being near him, and he knew it.

"Stay close," M muttered under his breath, forcing calm into his voice as they entered the airport.

E and Susie nodded, their pace quickening as they followed M. He led the way, expertly weaving through the throngs of travelers, his eyes constantly darting to the sides, ensuring they stayed out of sight. Every step they took toward the gate felt like a countdown, a race against time before the hunters spotted their prey.

By the time they reached the gate, M's chest felt tight. He knew he couldn't keep this up. E and Susie had a chance to get out of this alive, but as long as he stayed with them, he was a walking target. The men in the terminal weren't here for E—they were here for him.

As the boarding process began, M hesitated, his mind racing. Turning to E and Susie, he forced a casual tone. "Look, I think it's better if we split up. I'll take the train to Cape Town and meet you there. It's safer if we're not all in one place."

E immediately frowned, his brow furrowing with concern. "What? No way, M. We stick together. That's the plan."

"E's right," Susie chimed in, crossing her arms defiantly. "Splitting up is the worst thing we could do right now."

M sighed, running a hand through his hair, frustration and guilt gnawing at him. He could see the worry etched on their faces, but he couldn't let them convince him otherwise. "Fine," he relented. "I'll board with you, but I need to hit the bathroom first. I'll meet you on the plane."

E nodded reluctantly, grabbing Susie's arm and guiding her toward the gate. M watched as they disappeared into the jetway, his heart pounding harder with each step they took away from him.

As soon as they were out of sight, M turned on his heel and began retracing his steps, slipping out of the terminal with practiced ease. He kept his head low, blending into the flow of passengers, moving quickly but deliberately. Outside, he flagged down a cab parked near the entrance, his movements calm despite the adrenaline surging through his veins.

"Where to?" the driver asked.

"Anywhere but here," M muttered as he climbed into the backseat, slamming the door behind him.

Meanwhile, aboard the plane, E and Susie settled into their seats, their eyes darting to the cabin entrance, expecting M to appear at any moment. As the minutes ticked by and the flight attendants began preparing for takeoff, E's unease grew.

"Where the hell is he?" E muttered, shifting in his seat.

Susie glanced at him, her face pale with worry. "Maybe he's stuck in the boarding line?"

But deep down, they both knew. As the plane taxied down the runway and lifted into the air, E clenched his fists, staring out the window with a mixture of anger and dread.

M was gone.

For E and Susie, the uncertainty was maddening. Where had M gone? What had happened? Was he alive? These questions would gnaw at them for the entire flight, leaving them with nothing but anxiety and speculation.

But for M, there was no time to dwell on regret or second-guess his decision. As the cab sped away from the airport, he knew he had done what was necessary. Keeping E and Susie alive meant removing himself from the equation, even if it meant facing the danger alone.

THE EMBASSY

Out of options and running out of time, M directed the cab driver toward the US Embassy in Johannesburg. He knew it was a long shot—borderline desperate—but it was the only idea he had left. As the cab weaved through the city's streets, M sat in the backseat, his thoughts racing. He had no appointment, no connections, no guarantees, but he clung to the hope that someone—anyone—inside the embassy would listen.

When the cab pulled up in front of the heavily fortified embassy, M handed over the fare and stepped out onto the sidewalk. The air was thick with tension, and the looming presence of security cameras and armed guards didn't help. Taking a deep breath, M walked toward the main gate where two local guards stood watch, their PKMs slung across their chests.

One of the guards raised a hand to stop him. "What do you want?" he asked curtly, his tone more bored than concerned.

"I need to speak with another American," M said firmly, his voice steady despite the nerves knotting his stomach. "This is an emergency. I just need to talk to an American."

The guard's expression didn't change. "Do you have an appointment?"

"No, I don't," M admitted, "but this is urgent. It's a matter of life and death."

The guard sighed, visibly annoyed. He gestured lazily toward an intercom mounted on the wall nearby. "Try your luck there," he said dismissively.

M clenched his jaw but held his temper. He walked to the intercom, pressed the button, and waited. A voice crackled through the speaker after a moment—a voice with a heavy South African accent. It was clear the person on the other end wasn't an American.

"I need to speak with an American," M insisted. "It's an emergency. It's about the safety of another American—a veteran."

The voice on the intercom remained skeptical, pushing back with bureaucratic responses and vague reassurances. M's frustration grew, but he kept his composure, explaining and reexplaining the urgency of his request. Each passing minute felt like an eternity, but he refused to back down.

Finally, after over an hour of pleading and arguing, the heavy gates creaked open. A man in a cheap suit emerged, his expression wary as he approached. "Follow me," he said, motioning for M to enter.

Inside, the man led M to a small, nondescript room. The atmosphere was sterile, the walls bare except for a large American flag and a photo of the president. Sitting across from the embassy staffer, M tried to explain the situation without revealing too much. He spoke in hushed tones, detailing the bounty on his head and the organization pursuing him. Most importantly, he begged for help securing a safe flight for E and Susie to escape the country.

The staffer listened, his expression unreadable until M mentioned the name of the organization. In that instant, a flicker of fear crossed the man's face—a brief but unmistakable reaction.

"We don't have the kind of security to deal with that level of threat," the man finally said, his voice low and grave. "If what you're saying is true, you're on your own. We can't risk getting involved."

M's heart sank. "You don't understand," he said urgently. "I'm not asking for much—just a way to get E and Susie out of here safely."

The staffer shook his head, already standing up. "I'm sorry. There's nothing more we can do. You need to leave—quickly."

Before M could protest further, the man ushered him out of the room and back toward the gates. The heavy iron doors groaned open once more, and M found himself back on the street, alone.

As the gates clanged shut behind him, M stood there for a moment, staring at the embassy's imposing façade. The weight of the rejection pressed down on him, but he didn't have time to dwell on it. He needed a new plan—and fast.

With the sun dipping lower in the sky, he flagged down another cab, his mind racing with possibilities. He didn't know where to go next, but one thing was certain: he couldn't stop moving.

A FRIEND AND A VIOLENT WELCOME

As M left the embassy, feeling the weight of rejection and fear pressing on him, he decided to seek refuge with someone he hoped he could trust. He and E had befriended a young local lawyer during their time in Johannesburg—a man who lived with his parents and sister in a modest house on the outskirts of the city. The lawyer had been kind and generous in the past, and while M didn't have his phone number, he remembered where he lived. It was a risk, but at this point, he didn't have many options.

Directing the cab driver through the quiet streets of the suburbs, M's mind raced with uncertainty. Would his friend be home? Would he even be willing to help, knowing the danger that followed M? When the cab finally pulled up in front of the residence, M took a deep breath, handed over the fare, and stepped out onto the dusty street.

The house was surrounded by a high, solid wall topped with shards of broken glass—a common but unnerving sight in Johannesburg. M approached the gate and rang the bell. Moments later, his friend emerged from the house, walking briskly toward the gate with a pleasant smile.

"M!" he exclaimed warmly, opening the gate without hesitation. "Come in, come in!"

M stepped inside, and his friend immediately closed the gate behind him, locking it securely. As they walked toward the house, the lawyer's demeanor shifted slightly, the smile fading as he glanced around nervously. "I heard about what happened," he said quietly, his tone serious. "There's a lot of people gunning for you right now. If you need a place to stay, you're more than welcome to stay the night here."

Relief washed over M. He hadn't even needed to ask. For the first time in hours, he felt a small sense of safety. He nodded gratefully. "Thank you, brother. I really appreciate it."

Inside the house, M was introduced to the rest of the family—the lawyer's parents and younger sister. The house was modest, with two bedrooms, a garage, and a single bathroom. Despite its size, the property was well-maintained, with a neatly trimmed yard behind the high walls. Iron bars secured every window and door, and even the walls of the house had gun ports built into them.

Curious about the level of security, M asked, "Why so much fortification?"

His friend let out a nervous laugh. "Because at least once a month, someone tries to break in. If they get in…we all die."

The statement hung in the air, heavy with grim reality. After a moment, his friend continued, "If something happens tonight, I'll show you where the rifles are. We'll need every hand we can get. Shoot anything that moves if it comes over that wall."

M nodded without hesitation. "Copy that. I've got you, brother."

Fighting off intruders wasn't new to M. He had defended compounds before, and he was no stranger to high-stakes battles. Despite the ominous warning, he didn't let fear get to him. After sharing beers and talking late into the night, M and the family retreated to their respective sleeping areas. M lay down on a cot in the garage, exhaustion quickly overtaking him.

Around 2:00 a.m., his peace was shattered by shouts outside. Bright floodlights suddenly illuminated the yard, and his friend's voice rang out, sharp and urgent: "Get to the guns!"

M sprang out of bed, adrenaline pumping as he grabbed one of the Mosin-Nagants the family had stored in the garage. Racing to a window, he peered out and immediately spotted the source of the commotion. Old, ragged mattresses had been thrown over the broken glass at the top of the wall, and men armed with machetes, clubs, and guns were scaling the barrier. They poured into the yard like a relentless tide, their intentions unmistakably violent.

It was like a scene from a nightmare—a horde of attackers surging forward, their shadows twisting in the harsh light. Without hesitation, M opened fire, each shot landing with lethal precision. The cracks of gunfire from the rest of the family echoed around him, everyone defending their home with a ferocity born of desperation.

The attackers kept coming, pressing closer and closer to the house. M could feel the weight of the fight—the sheer number of them—threatening to overwhelm their defenses. His breaths came fast and hard as he fired shot after shot, his focus unyielding.

Just as it seemed the tide might turn against them, the deep, thunderous *thud-thud-thud* of a heavy machine gun filled the air. The unmistakable sound of a *DShK*—a heavy machine gun mounted on a vehicle—echoed through the night, rattling the ground beneath their feet. Massive rounds slammed into the walls and the attackers, tearing apart the chaotic advance. Bits of stucco, broken glass, and debris flew into the air as the overwhelming firepower obliterated the attackers' resolve.

M ducked instinctively as the noise reverberated through the yard. Glancing toward the street, he caught sight of a vehicle with the bold ADT logo emblazoned on its side. It was a roving patrol truck, part of the neighborhood's private security service, responding just in time to save them from being overrun. The machine gun was mounted on the back of the truck operated by a security officer who was firing with terrifying accuracy.

The attackers froze, their bravado evaporating as the onslaught tore into their ranks. Panic rippled through the group as they began retreating, scrambling back over the walls and out of the yard. The floodlights illuminated their desperate flight, and their once-coordinated assault turned into a chaotic retreat.

As the heavy machine gun continued its suppressive fire, something unexpected happened: the neighbors emerged. Doors creaked open up and down the street, and men and women, armed with whatever they could find, began pouring into the fight. Some carried hunting rifles, others wielded machetes or clubs. A few older children even held slingshots, ready to defend their families and homes.

M could see the resolve in their faces—these people weren't just defending his friend's family; they were defending their entire community. Shots rang out from all directions as neighbors fired at the fleeing attackers, their shouts mingling with the distant roar of the machine gun.

One of the neighbors, an older man with a hunting rifle, leaned over the wall near M's position and grinned grimly. "They picked the wrong neighborhood tonight," he said, letting loose another round toward the retreating figures.

M nodded, reloading his rifle and scanning the yard for any remaining threats. The attackers had fully retreated now, disappearing into the darkness beyond the walls. The only sounds left were the crackling of the floodlights, the distant rumble of the ADT truck's engine, and the nervous murmurs of neighbors gathering to assess the aftermath.

Breathing heavily, M lowered his rifle and looked at his friend. "That was close," he said, his voice calm but tinged with relief.

"Too close," his friend replied, still gripping his rifle tightly. "If ADT hadn't shown up when they did..." He trailed off, shaking his head as he stared at the yard, now littered with broken glass, torn clothing, and abandoned weapons.

The ADT security officer with the machine gun dismounted from the truck and approached the group, his expression grim but professional. "You folks okay?" he asked, his eyes scanning the property.

"We are now," M's friend said, nodding. "Thanks to you."

The officer gave a short nod. "We'll do a sweep of the area to make sure they're gone. If anything happens, call us immediately."

As the officer returned to the truck, the neighbors began exchanging quiet thanks and reassurances, their bond strengthened by the night's events. M looked around at the tired but determined faces and felt a strange sense of camaraderie. These people had risked their lives not just for themselves, but for each other.

When the neighbors finally began retreating to their homes and the ADT truck rumbled away into the night, M turned to his friend. "Thanks for taking me in, brother. I didn't expect this kind of welcome."

His friend laughed softly, though there was still a nervous edge to it. "This is Johannesburg, M. You never know what's coming, but we always stand together."

M nodded, exhaustion finally catching up with him. "Let's hope they don't come back. I'm too damn tired for a second round."

The two men exchanged a weary smile before heading back into the house. For now, the danger had passed, but M knew it was only a matter of time before it returned. In a city like this, safety was never guaranteed, but tonight, against all odds, they had survived—and that was enough.

FROM BAD TO WORSE

The next morning, M sat on the worn couch in his friend's modest living room, the sunlight filtering through the iron-barred windows. The television flickered with the morning news, and M barely paid attention at first, his mind still clouded by exhaustion and the events of the night before. But then the anchor's words caught his ear, and the images on the screen made his heart plummet.

A *Mango Airlines flight* had crashed near Cape Town. There were no survivors.

M's breath caught in his throat. His heart began to race as he stared at the wreckage on the screen—charred metal twisted into unrecognizable shapes, smoke still rising in the morning light. The flight details blurred together in his mind as a cold realization gripped him. E and Susie. They had flown to Cape Town the day before.

"No," he whispered, shaking his head in disbelief. His hands trembled as he grabbed his phone, desperately dialing E's number. The phone rang and rang, each unanswered tone twisting the knife in his chest a little deeper. "Pick up, E," he muttered, his voice cracking. "Pick up."

But there was no answer.

He tried again. And again. Nothing.

M's stomach churned, his palms slick with sweat as the reality began to set in. "This can't be," he whispered, his voice barely audible. "That wasn't supposed to happen."

A profound emptiness began to engulf him, a black hole swallowing his thoughts, his strength, his hope. E and Susie were gone. He was alone now—truly, completely alone. The weight of it crushed him, and for a moment, he couldn't breathe.

After a long silence, he stood, forcing himself to move. He turned to his friend and his family, offering a weak smile that didn't reach his eyes. "Thank you for everything," he said, his voice hollow. He embraced them each in turn, his gratitude genuine but overshadowed by his grief.

With nothing left to say, he stepped out onto the street, the warm Johannesburg sun doing little to thaw the cold emptiness in his chest. He didn't know where he was going or what he was going to do. He had no money, no plan, and no one to turn to. His heart felt like it had been shattered into a million pieces, held together only by scars and the agony bursting within him.

He walked.

The hours passed, the city's noise and chaos fading into the background as his feet carried him forward without direction or purpose. The sun began to set, painting the sky in shades of orange and pink, but M barely noticed. Eventually, he found a dense patch of brush and crawled into it, curling up on the hard ground. His sleep that night was restless, filled with fragmented nightmares and the aching void left by his loss.

When the first rays of dawn broke through the trees, M stirred, his body stiff and aching. He stood, brushing the dirt from his clothes, and began walking again.

By the second day, he had wandered out of the city, the urban sprawl giving way to open countryside. He didn't know what direction he was going or how far he had come. His mind was clouded by hunger and dehydration, his thoughts spiraling into a fog of despair. He walked all day, his feet blistered and raw, the pain dulled only by his overwhelming grief. That night, he found a drainage ditch and lay down inside, the cold concrete pressing against his back as he tried to sleep.

The next morning, he woke with the first light, his body screaming for food and water. He pushed forward, his legs moving on autopilot. By midafternoon, his vision began to blur, and he stumbled along the side of a dirt road, his body threatening to give out.

The sound of an engine pulled him from his daze. A flatbed truck slowed to a stop beside him, the dust kicking up into the air as the driver leaned out of the window. M didn't even look up at first, his mind too foggy to process what was happening.

Then he heard the voice.

"What the fuck, M? Is that you?"

M lifted his head, squinting against the sunlight. His heart skipped a beat as recognition dawned. Sitting in the driver's seat, grinning in disbelief, was one of the men from the South African Recce Bar—the same bar he, Johan, E, and J had visited weeks before.

The man jumped down from the truck, his boots crunching on the dirt as he approached. "Jesus, M, you look like hell," he said, clapping a hand on M's shoulder. "What the hell are you doing out here?"

M opened his mouth to reply, but the words wouldn't come. His knees buckled, and the man caught him, steadying him with a firm grip.

"Easy, mate. Let's get you in the truck," the man said, guiding him toward the passenger seat. "We'll get you sorted out."

As the truck rumbled back to life and began to move, M leaned back in the seat, his body too weak to resist. For the first time in days, a flicker of hope sparked within him. Maybe he wasn't as alone as he thought.

GET READY

M still wore the old South African Recce uniform that Johan had given him several weeks ago. The fabric was now even more tattered and worn, stained with blood, sweat, and dirt—a testament to the battles fought and hardships endured. It clung to him like a second skin, no longer just a piece of clothing but a part of him, a symbol of survival and perseverance. In some strange way, he felt it was a badge of honor, a tribute to the departed soldier who had once worn it.

Now, riding in the flatbed truck alongside battle-hardened South African soldiers, M felt a flicker of purpose returning to his hollow chest. These men, scarred by conflict and shaped by years of relentless struggle, radiated a quiet confidence that was both intimidating and comforting. They moved with the fluidity of those who had faced death countless times and lived to tell the tale.

As the truck bounced over the rough road, one of the soldiers handed M a canteen of water and a small packet of food. M accepted it gratefully, taking long gulps from the canteen before tearing into the food. It was simple—dried meat and a piece of bread—but it tasted like a feast to someone who hadn't eaten in days.

Curious about their mission, M asked, "What are you guys doing out here?"

The man sitting closest to him, a grizzled veteran with a scar running down the side of his face, let out a heavy sigh. His eyes, weathered and sharp, met M's with a gravity that made the air around them feel heavier. "We're heading to the farms," he said. "There've been reports of machete gangs attacking farmers en masse. Entire families slaughtered, crops burned to ash, livestock butchered. It's a massacre out there."

M felt a chill run down his spine as he listened. The weight of the words hung in the air, the imagery vivid and horrifying.

The man continued, his voice grim but resolute. "The police won't go out there. Too dangerous. Too remote. So, we're going to see if we can put a stop to it."

M sat silently for a moment, digesting what he'd just heard. These weren't just random skirmishes—this was wholesale slaughter, a campaign of terror aimed at driving families from their land or wiping them out entirely. He felt a surge of anger and a pang of empathy for the victims. He had nothing left—no family, no direction, no plan. But these men, and their mission, offered something he desperately needed: a chance to stand for something again.

"Can I join you?" M asked, his voice steady despite the storm of emotions churning inside him.

The man glanced at him, measuring him with a careful gaze. Then with a faint smile, he said, "Absolutely. We need everyone we can get. From what I hear, this is going to be one hell of a fight."

M straightened in his seat, a mixture of adrenaline and uncertainty coursing through him. He didn't know what lay ahead, and perhaps that was for the best. If he'd known the horrors and trials that awaited him in the days to come, he might have wished for the peace of death instead.

As the truck rumbled on, the landscape around them shifted from the outskirts of the city to the vast, sprawling farmland. The air grew quieter, heavier with the anticipation of violence. M clenched his fists, the rough fabric of the uniform grounding him as he steeled himself for whatever was to come.

For the first time in what felt like an eternity, he had a purpose, a reason to keep moving. But as the truck neared its destination, the grim reality of their mission became clearer. This wasn't just another fight—this was survival, justice, and vengeance rolled into one, and M was about to be thrust into the heart of it.

A LOOK INTO HELL

After spending most of the day traveling in the truck, the group neared their destination. The once-serene farmlands began to change, the vibrant greens and golds of the fields giving way to plumes of black smoke rising ominously in the distance. The smell of burning vegetation and charred flesh began to seep into the truck, making every man tense with dread.

As they crested a small hill, the devastation came into full view. Fields lay smoldering, crops reduced to ash, and the bodies of livestock were strewn across the pastures in grotesque positions. The driver of the truck let out a sharp gasp, his voice cracking as he whispered, "That's my sister's house…my sister lives there!"

Panic overtook him as he slammed his foot down on the accelerator, the truck lurching forward with a sudden burst of speed. The men in the back held on tightly, their eyes wide with growing fear as they neared the farmhouse. The closer they got, the worse it became. The yard was littered with debris—broken tools, charred wood, and things too horrific to identify.

The truck screeched to a halt in the front yard, dust and ash swirling around them. Before it had fully stopped, the men leapt from the vehicle, their weapons drawn and their senses on high alert. M stepped onto the ground, his boots crunching against the blood-soaked dirt. His eyes were immediately drawn to a large cast-iron pot sitting over smoldering logs in the middle of the yard.

It looked like something out of a twisted fairytale—a witch's cauldron, grotesque and foreboding. There was something about it that made M's stomach churn, a deep, instinctual warning screaming at him not to look. But he couldn't stop himself. Slowly, he approached the pot, his breath shallow and his heart pounding.

As he peered over the blackened rim, the sight inside made his knees buckle. The contents of the pot were so horrific, so unspeakably vile, that tears instantly welled up in his eyes. He stumbled back, his mind reeling, bile rising in his throat. Whatever innocence he had left was obliterated in that moment. Two small children lay boiled in a mix of what looked like used motor oil. Their little bodies blistered and burned.

Before he could fully process what he'd seen, his attention was drawn to the farmhouse. The truck's driver was sprinting toward the front porch, his panic palpable. M's eyes darted to the blood—bright red streaks running down the steps, pooling in the yard, now darkening under the relentless African sun. Without hesitation, M and the other men followed, their weapons ready but their minds gripped by dread over what they might find inside.

As they burst through the front door, the sickly metallic smell of blood hit them like a wall. The floorboards were slick, nearly sending M sprawling as he tried to keep his footing. Blood was everywhere—splattered across the walls, smeared along the floors, and dripping from furniture. The men moved with purpose, but no one spoke, their silence a testament to the terror gripping their hearts.

The driver didn't bother clearing the house—he knew exactly where to go. He sprinted into the kitchen, his boots splashing in puddles of blood, and then came the sound that froze everyone in their tracks.

A shriek.

Not a cry, not a scream, but a soul-wrenching, primal sound filled with unimaginable pain and anguish. It ripped through the house, making every man's heart stop.

M and the others rushed into the kitchen, and what they saw made time itself seem to freeze.

The scene was grotesque, beyond anything they could have imagined. The air was heavy with the stench of death, the walls painted with violent, chaotic streaks of blood. M's vision blurred as he tried to process the horror in front of him, his mind rejecting the details even as they seared themselves into his memory. A female lay stretched out on the kitchen table, her hands and feet nailed to the wooden table. Her chest was ripped open and her entrails lay strewn about the small kitchen. What M assumed was her husband was naked, wrapped in barbed wire hanging from a chain from the kitchen ceiling. He was dead, but M could see his eyelids had been cut off. Forcing him to watch the horrors committed on his wife before he had his private parts ripped or cut off and left to bleed out.

The driver dropped to his knees, his body trembling as he reached out to the shattered remnants of his family. His sobs filled the room, raw and guttural, each one carving deeper wounds into the men around him.

M staggered back, gripping the door frame for support. His breath came in short, shallow gasps as his heart pounded in his chest. He wanted to look away, to shield himself from the unspeakable carnage, but he couldn't. This wasn't just an act of violence—it was a message, a display of pure, unfiltered evil.

One of the other men whispered, his voice shaking, "Who…who does this? What kind of monsters—"

"Focus!" barked the scarred veteran, cutting him off. His voice, though steady, carried a tremor of rage. "We need to secure the property. There might still be survivors—or worse, those bastards might still be here."

The men nodded, snapping back to the task at hand, though their faces betrayed the storm of emotions inside them. M swallowed hard, his fingers tightening around his rifle as he forced himself to move. He couldn't afford to break down—not now.

But as they spread out through the house and the surrounding property, searching for survivors or any sign of the attackers, one thing became painfully clear: the family was gone. Every member had been slaughtered, their lives stolen in the most brutal and senseless way imaginable.

By the time the search was over, the men regrouped in the yard, their faces pale and drawn. The driver sat on the porch steps, his head in his hands, the weight of his loss pressing down on him like a physical force.

M stood nearby, his rifle still in hand, his knuckles white as he gripped it tightly. The rage bubbling inside him threatened to spill over, but he forced himself to stay calm. This wasn't over. Whoever had done this was still out there, and they needed to be stopped.

For M, this wasn't just another tragedy. It was a turning point, a moment that would shape the battles to come. He wasn't just fighting to survive anymore—he was fighting for justice, for vengeance, and for every innocent life that had been stolen by the monsters they were up against.

IT'S NOT OVER

As the men stood in the front yard, their faces grim with exhaustion and grief, a plume of dust appeared on the horizon. It moved swiftly, growing larger with every passing second. One of the soldiers raised his rifle and peered through the scope, his jaw tightening as he focused.

"Shit," he muttered under his breath. "The bastards are coming back."

Every man snapped to attention, their instincts kicking in. "Get ready, boys!" the soldier barked, his voice steady despite the rising tension. The men scrambled to the truck, grabbing the remaining weapons and ammunition before sprinting back to the farmhouse. They barricaded the doors and reinforced the windows as best as they could, knowing the fight ahead would push them to their limits.

The dust cloud grew closer, revealing the vehicles within. Six trucks came into view, each packed with armed men. One was a flatbed carrying at least twenty fighters, their weapons glinting in the harsh sunlight.

M and the South African Recce soldiers moved methodically, taking up defensive positions inside the farmhouse. They distributed the ammunition evenly among themselves, each man acutely aware that every bullet counted. The mood inside the house was tense but resolute. Fury and a burning sense of vengeance radiated from their eyes as they watched the convoy approach.

The trucks slowed as they neared the farmhouse, splitting off and forming a semicircle around the front of the property. Dust settled as the vehicles stopped, and men began bailing out, taking up positions behind the trucks and scattered debris.

Then the gunfire began.

The first volley was deafening, a thunderous roar of chaos as bullets tore into the farmhouse. Wood splintered, glass shattered, and walls groaned under the relentless assault. The air was thick with the acrid smell of gunpowder and the sharp sounds of ricochets.

M and the soldiers fired back with ruthless precision. Each shot was deliberate, aimed with the calm efficiency of seasoned fighters. Bodies dropped outside as their rounds found their marks, but the attackers kept advancing, undeterred by their losses.

"Keep it together!" shouted one of the Recce men, his voice cutting through the cacophony.

Suddenly, a cry erupted from across the room. "I'm hit! I'm hit!"

M's head snapped toward the sound. One of the soldiers was slumped against the wall, his shoulder torn apart by a round, his arm barely hanging on by sinew and skin. Without hesitation, M sprang into action.

He grabbed the med kit and slid across the blood-streaked floor to the injured man. "Hold still!" he barked, his hands steady despite the chaos around them. He tore open a packet of quick clot and pressed it into the wound, ignoring the soldier's groans of pain. Next, he secured an Israeli bandage around the mangled shoulder and reached into the med bag for a syringe.

"This'll keep you in the fight," M said, injecting the soldier with a shot of adrenaline. The man's eyes widened as the drug took effect, his breathing stabilizing despite the pain.

"Thank you," the soldier mumbled, his voice weak but grateful.

"Stay down," M ordered before returning to his position at the window. He reloaded his rifle, popped up, and fired three quick, precise shots, dropping another group of attackers. The assault outside showed no signs of letting up.

After two and a half grueling hours of continuous combat, the farmhouse was a scene of devastation. The men inside were battered and bloodied, their numbers now reduced to three. Five of their comrades lay lifeless on the blood-soaked floor, their bodies riddled with shrapnel and bullet holes. The walls of the house were perforated with so many bullet holes that it seemed a miracle it still stood.

Outside, the attackers regrouped. Reinforcements arrived—two additional truckloads of fighters. The horde was larger now, more determined, and better equipped.

Inside the farmhouse, M and the two remaining soldiers counted their ammunition. Between them, they had only a handful of rounds left—six, maybe seven shots at most. It wasn't enough.

"Search the house!" one of the soldiers barked, his voice tight with desperation. "Anything we can use—knives, tools, anything!"

M frantically rifled through the debris-strewn kitchen, coming up with a butcher knife and a heavy iron pan. Another soldier found a hatchet, while the third grabbed a rusted crowbar from the garage. It wasn't much, but it would have to do.

The three men retreated to the stairway leading up to the second floor, their final fallback position. They stacked overturned furniture at the base of the stairs, creating a makeshift barricade. Each man gripped their improvised weapons tightly, their eyes fixed on the front door as the attackers outside began to close in.

"This is it," one of the soldiers said quietly, his voice steady but tinged with grim acceptance.

M nodded, his jaw clenched. "If they want us, they'll have to come through hell to get us."

The silence outside was almost more terrifying than the gunfire. The attackers were regrouping, preparing for a final push. M tightened his grip on the butcher knife, his knuckles white. His body was exhausted, his mind screaming for rest, but his resolve was unshakable.

The sound of boots crunching on gravel signaled the approaching horde. Then came the crash—a battering ram slamming into the barricaded front door.

"This is it," M whispered to himself, his heart pounding as the door began to splinter.

The fight for survival wasn't over. It was just beginning.

As the front door burst open, the attackers outside let out a guttural, bloodthirsty scream: *"Kill the boer!"* Their voices were filled with rage, their intent unmistakable. They surged through the narrow doorway in a chaotic wave, weapons raised, their eyes burning with murderous intent.

At the base of the staircase, the three defenders stood ready, their improvised weapons clenched tightly in their hands. What followed was a savage and relentless onslaught—a desperate, hand-to-hand fight for survival. The small entryway exploded into chaos as fists, blades, and blunt objects clashed violently.

M fought with the raw, primal fury of a cornered animal. He didn't have time to think—only to react. His world shrank to the few feet of space around him, each swing of his knife driven by pure adrenaline. Every move was instinctual, his survival mechanisms firing on all cylinders. Blood splattered the walls, and the room filled with grunts, screams, and the sickening sounds of steel meeting flesh.

The attackers tried to pour into the house, but the narrow doorway became a bottleneck. Their numbers, which should have been their advantage, now worked against them. Bodies began piling up as M and the two South African soldiers fought with everything they had. Each swing of a hatchet, each thrust of a knife pushed the attackers back just enough to keep the defenders alive.

The sheer ferocity of the fight seemed to unnerve the attackers. The men inside the house fought with a level of desperation that bordered on madness, and every second that passed worked in their favor. The doorway became clogged with bodies—some dead, others writhing in pain. The attackers outside had to climb over their fallen comrades to press forward, making them easy targets for the defenders.

The fight dragged on, a grueling twenty-five to thirty minutes of unrelenting violence. The three defenders were pushed to the brink, their muscles burning, their breaths ragged, their bodies battered and bleeding. But somehow, they held their ground.

And then, for reasons unknown, the attackers began to falter. The men outside hesitated, their shouts growing quieter, their movements less coordinated. Perhaps it was the sight of their comrades' bodies stacked in the doorway, or maybe it was the sheer endurance and ferocity of the defenders. Whatever the reason, their will to fight broke.

One by one, the attackers retreated, scrambling back to their vehicles. The roar of engines filled the air as the trucks sped away into the darkness, leaving the farmhouse eerily quiet.

Inside, M and the two remaining soldiers collapsed onto the pile of bodies at the base of the stairs. Their weapons slipped from their trembling hands as they gasped for air, their chests heaving with exhaustion. Their muscles burned with lactic acid, their cuts and wounds stinging, but they were too drained to move. Blood—some theirs, some not—covered their bodies, soaking into their clothes.

They lay there in the silence, gripping each other's hands, their adrenaline still coursing through their veins. The weight of what they had just survived began to sink in, but there was no relief, no victory. The night was now pitch black, and an unnatural stillness had settled over the farm.

The usual sounds of the African night—chirping insects, rustling leaves, the distant calls of animals—were conspicuously absent. It was as if even nature itself recoiled from the horrors that had unfolded on this property. The silence was oppressive, almost deafening, and it wrapped around the house like a shroud.

In that moment, the farm felt like the very depths of hell. The air was heavy with the stench of blood and death, the ground slick with gore. The three men were alive, but their survival felt like a hollow victory. They were broken, battered, and haunted by the carnage around them.

As the hours stretched on, the silence persisted, a grim reminder of the horrors they had endured. And though the attackers had retreated, the men inside the farmhouse knew that they would never truly escape the nightmare of this night.

As the three men lay motionless in the aftermath, M's body finally gave out. Whether he passed out from exhaustion or drifted into a restless sleep, he wasn't sure. His dreams, if they could even be called that, were a tangled web of blood and screams, replaying the horrors of the night in vivid, fractured detail.

When the first rays of sunlight crested the horizon, piercing through the broken windows of the farmhouse, M stirred. His muscles screamed in protest as he forced himself to sit up, every joint stiff and aching. The two other survivors, equally battered and drained, slowly roused themselves, exchanging silent glances that conveyed the shared weight of their trauma.

They staggered out into the front yard, the light of day revealing the full extent of the carnage they had fought through. Blood soaked the ground, pooling in the dirt and mixing with ash. Bodies, twisted and broken, lay strewn across the yard, their lifeless eyes staring blankly at the sky. The air was thick with the smell of death, mingling with the metallic tang of dried blood and the acrid scent of smoldering wood.

The scene was beyond comprehension, a tableau of violence and inhumanity that defied explanation. For a long moment, the men just stood there, their minds struggling to process the sight before them.

Finally, one of the soldiers broke the silence. "We can't leave them like this," he said, his voice hoarse and heavy with grief.

M nodded, his throat too dry to speak. He and the others set to work, gathering the remains of their fallen comrades and what was left of the family who had once called this farmhouse home. It was slow, grueling work, each body a grim reminder of the life that had been stolen.

They dug graves in the hard, unyielding earth, the effort taxing their already-depleted strength. The morning sun climbed higher in the sky, its relentless heat bearing down on them as they labored in silence. Sweat and tears mingled as they carved out final resting places for their friends, their comrades, and the innocent family who had been caught in the crossfire of cruelty.

By midday, the graves were finished. M and the others placed simple wooden crosses above each, marking the spots where lives had ended too soon. Standing over the graves, they bowed their heads, not in prayer—none of them had the strength for that—but in solemn respect.

The bodies of the attackers, however, were left where they had fallen. The men agreed silently that they deserved no more than to become carrion for the vultures already circling overhead. It was a brutal but fitting end for those who had brought death and destruction to this place.

With their grim task complete, the three men climbed into one of the remaining vehicles in the yard. The engine sputtered to life, breaking the oppressive silence as they began their journey back to Johannesburg. None of them spoke; there were no words for what they had endured, no way to make sense of the horrors they had witnessed. Each man was locked in his own thoughts, trying and failing to wrap his mind around how human beings could be so cruel, so devoid of compassion.

M slumped in the passenger seat, his gaze fixed on the horizon but seeing nothing. His heart felt like a hollow, aching void, every shred of light and hope stripped away. He thought of the family who had welcomed him, their warm smiles and generous spirits now extinguished forever. He thought of the comrades who had fought and died by his side, their sacrifices etched into his soul.

As the miles rolled by, a new pit of despair opened within him. It felt endless, a dark abyss that threatened to swallow him whole. He didn't cry—he couldn't. There was nothing left inside him but a numbing, all-encompassing emptiness.

The farmhouse, the graves, the blood-soaked yard—it all felt like a nightmare that he would never wake up from. And as the vehicle carried them away from the scene of carnage, M couldn't shake the feeling that a part of him had died there, buried alongside those wooden crosses in the unforgiving soil.

LEAVING

As M and the two soldiers approached Johannesburg, the weight of the last forty-eight hours hung heavily in the air. The men had barely spoken since leaving the farmhouse, their silence filled with unspoken grief and exhaustion. The once-familiar outline of the city's skyline now seemed foreign to M, a stark reminder of how much his world had changed in such a short span of time.

One of the soldiers broke the silence, glancing at M from the driver's seat. "We'll help you get out of the country," he said, his voice steady but low. "We've heard about the bounty on your head. You've earned it, mate. After what you've been through, it's the least we can do."

M didn't respond immediately. His throat tightened as he turned to look at the soldier. A quiet nod was all he could muster, a simple gesture of gratitude for an offer that felt like a lifeline.

They drove him to a small, unmarked airport on the outskirts of the city. The airstrip was quiet, the hum of propellers and the occasional bark of orders from the staff the only sounds breaking the stillness. It was a stark contrast to the chaos and violence M had left behind, and the surreal calm of the place made it feel as though he were walking through a dream.

The soldiers parked the truck near the terminal and stepped out with M, their boots crunching on the gravel. One of them pulled M into a firm embrace, clapping him on the back. "You're a tough bastard," he said with a faint smile. "Wherever you go, don't let them forget that."

The other soldier extended his hand. "Stay safe, brother. And if you ever need help, you know where to find us."

M shook their hands, his grip firm despite the tremble in his fingers. "Thank you," he said, his voice hoarse. He didn't have the words to express the depth of his gratitude, but the look in his eyes said enough.

With a few parting nods, he turned and walked toward the terminal, his boots feeling heavier with each step. The soldiers watched him go, standing silently by the truck until he disappeared from view.

Inside, the process of boarding was a blur. He handed over what little identification he had, his name now reduced to a series of stamps and papers hastily prepared for his escape. He moved through security, each step feeling like it brought him closer to something—but what, he couldn't say.

When he finally settled into his seat on the plane, he let out a shaky breath. As the engines roared to life and the aircraft began its ascent, M rested his head against the cool glass of the window. Below him, the sprawling landscape of South Africa faded into the distance, giving way to the endless expanse of ocean.

He watched the waves far below, their rhythmic patterns a stark contrast to the chaos that had consumed his life. For the first time in days, he felt a moment of quiet, but it wasn't peace—it was an eerie stillness, as if his mind had gone numb to protect him from the weight of his memories.

He didn't know what would come next. How could he? The future stretched out before him like the ocean beneath the plane—vast, uncharted, and unknowable. How would he explain the horrors he'd seen? How would he live with the images and scars now permanently etched into his mind?

The faces of the family at the farmhouse flickered in his memory. The friends he'd fought beside, their laughter, their bravery, and their final moments. The blood, the screams, the silence that followed. It all played out in his head like a nightmare he couldn't escape.

But whatever lay ahead, M knew he had two choices: face it or let it break him.

As the plane leveled out, its engines droning softly, he closed his eyes. He didn't sleep, but he allowed himself to drift, his thoughts swirling as the weight of his journey pressed down on him. This chapter of his life had ended—abruptly, violently—but a new one was about to begin.

And though he couldn't yet see what that chapter held, he resolved to survive it. Because if he'd learned one thing in the depths of chaos and despair, it was this: survival wasn't just about enduring. It was about finding meaning in the scars and living to honor the ones who couldn't.

www.ingramcontent.com/pod-product-compliance
Lightning Source LLC
Chambersburg PA
CBHW031646040426
42453CB00006B/231